A Place to Cycle

Amazing rides from
around the world

Rob Penn

A Place to Cycle

Amazing rides from
around the world

To Mannanan

Published in 2005 by Conran Octopus Limited
a part of Octopus Publishing Group
2–4 Heron Quays, London E14 4JP
www.conran-octopus.co.uk
Reprinted in 2006

British Library Cataloguing-in-Publication Data.
A catalogue record for this book is available from
the British Library.

ISBN 10: 1-84091-391-6
ISBN 13: 978-1-84091-391-0

Publishing Director: Lorraine Dickey
Commissioning Editor: Katey Day
Editor: Sybella Marlow
Designer: Victoria Burley
Picture Research Manager: Liz Boyd
Picture Researcher: Sarah Hopper
Production Manager: Angela Couchman

Printed in China

Contents

Introduction

The bicycle is a transport of delight. Whether you are easing from restaurant to restaurant through a French valley or flying down jeep tracks in the Himalayas, there is no better way to travel. Offer me any form of transport — from a palanquin to a Lear jet — and I will (nearly) always opt for a two-wheeled steed. Travelling by bike is the best way to view a landscape, engage with a culture, acquire an appetite and feel a sense of achievement. In short, it is the best way to catch the music of the earth.

In the three years it took me to ride some 40,000 km (24,000 miles) around the world, I was frequently amazed at the level of trust placed in me by local people from the 31 countries I crossed, simply because I was riding a bicycle. Trust leads to hospitality, on a purely practical level, but it is also a key to kinship and understanding. And in modern times, when we can be at least cursorily familiar with so much of the planet from an armchair, this is one of the greatest goals of travel.

This book describes 25 rides from all corners of the planet, from New Zealand's South Island to the Canadian Rockies, from St Petersburg to Patagonia. There is something here for every level of experience. In order to give you an idea of the challenge each one represents, the rides have been categorized as easy, moderate or strenuous. These categories take into account the level of fitness and the biking skills required, as well as a host of other relevant factors from altitude to daily temperatures. The type of surface — from tarmac roads to single-track — and the daily distances will give you further insights into the level of

difficulty of each ride. There are both guided and self-guided rides, and the contact details of the companies that organize them are given at the end of each chapter.

The daily schedules for each ride are merely a guide: all manner of things, in particular the weather, can affect these routes. Similarly, the distances and the cycling times (an estimate of the hours spent in the saddle, which does not include sightseeing, eating and so on) may vary.

No two rides in this book are remotely the same: one follows an ancient pilgrimage route across northern Spain, another crosses Zanskar and the highest motorable road pass on the planet, and yet another cruises through the Californian redwood forests. Some rides focus on the culture of a country, others on the food or the landscape, while some are simply about hammering downhill very, very fast. But they all share one thing: they are memorable. If you need any encouragement to get on your bike, you should find it here. Time is running out — go for a ride.

Linz to Vienna, Austria

- Route rating: easy
- On-road (predominantly tarmac cycle paths)
- 8 days/7 nights
- Dates: June to August

Think of Austria, and soaring peaks set in Tyrolean landscapes come to mind. This is reasonable enough: Austria is, after all, a country dominated by mountains. But it also has a broad, flat plain cut by the mighty Danube, perfect for a long, lazy bike ride.

This is no secret: the cycle path on the banks of the Danube draws hordes of like-minded tourists on two wheels every year (especially in spring and autumn — the best reason for going in summer), and it is easy to understand why. There is something powerfully therapeutic about pedalling alongside this great river; the section from Linz to Vienna is a strong contender for the most beautiful stretch of the Danube, and so rich is this major waterway's history that the banks are peppered with ancient villages, great abbeys, castles and palaces.

For most of its length the ride follows the Danube Cycle Path, an excellent, traffic-free, tarmac route that is kept in good repair. The week includes two optional opportunities to stretch your legs and climb hills (for great views of the river), but if you eschew these the entire ride is flat. The daily distances are small, leaving plenty of time to explore whatever catches your interest along the bank. A 'host' will meet you in the hotel in Linz on your first night, fit the bikes up and provide you with maps, trip notes and a

booklet full of information. The ride each day is unguided and your bags will be transported to the next hotel, where again the host will be waiting to greet you.

The accommodation — in a combination of modern hotels and family-owned establishments — reaches its apogee at the Hotel Stefanie in Vienna, where the ride finishes. The capital of modern Austria and magnificent seat of the Habsburg Empire is a place that drips with history and nostalgia. Most people come here expecting to find grand Habsburg palaces, white horses, heart-stopping slices of cream cake and café waiters wearing dinner jackets — and they are not disappointed. It really is like that. The city could be accused of trading on its past, but what a past! Its legacy is an extraordinary wealth of architectural treasures, one of the world's great art collections and world-class orchestras. It is also a very safe place. After a week easing along beside the placid might of the Danube — a very calming cycling experience — stately Vienna is the perfect place for a refined celebration.

THE HISTORIC TOWN OF ENNS

THE GRANDIOSE, BAROQUE ABBEY AT MELK

Day 1: Vienna to Linz

Transfer from Vienna airport to the railway station for the scenic train ride along the Danube to the provincial capital of Linz. Your host will meet you at the hotel, on the banks of the river near the main square, where there is time to prepare the bikes before a stroll around the city. Linz is steeped in history – it was a Roman port, an important medieval trading centre, the largest railway junction in the Habsburg Empire and the site of the massive Hermann Göring iron and steel works – and there are interesting Baroque buildings at every turn in the carefully preserved 'Altstadt'. The Hauptplatz or main square is a beautiful place to spend the evening sitting in one of the open-air cafés listening to a concert. The great composer Anton Bruckner lived for many years in Linz, and his legacy is a wealth of culture today.

Day 2: Linz to Enns
27 km (17 miles); 3 hours cycling

There is no hurry today (or on any day of this trip, for that matter), and with your route notes in hand you can linger in Linz as long as you like before setting off downstream along the left bank of the Danube. The Danube Cycle Path eases between parkland and the muscular river, away from the city and then through apple orchards and farmland, on quiet lanes. Mauthausen, the notorious slave labour camp established beside the Danube by the Third Reich, is a chilling place to stop. More beguiling is the approach to the walled town of Enns, perched on a low hill above the river and dominated from a distance by its medieval clock tower. Many of the attractive pastel-coloured buildings in the centre of the town have 16th-century façades that hide much older structures, for Enns is one of the most important historic centres on the Danube, as Roman and Celtic archaeological sites outside the walls attest. The hotel is just off the main square, another elegant public space full of cafés.

Day 3: Enns to Grein
40 km (25 miles); 3½ hours cycling

A short freewheel out of Enns brings you back to the banks of the river, where a bicycle-boat will ferry you the ten minutes to the opposite bank. The route wends through rolling countryside, flanked by meadows carpeted with wild flowers and orchards, and past tranquil, picturesque villages such as Arbing and Hütting. An optional detour — for fortress buffs and anyone who needs to stretch their legs a little more — climbs the hill to Klam Castle, which offers fine views of the sweep of the river. A swift descent brings you down to Grein, dominated by another impressive castle and home to the oldest theatre in Austria: a delight for Rococo enthusiasts.

Day 4: Grein to Melk
52 km (32 miles); 4 hours cycling

The tree-lined path continues along the right bank of the river this morning, through the villages of Freyenstein and Persenburg, with great views across the plains all the way to Ybbs, where you stop for lunch. The hillier left bank is dotted with castles, but the most imposing view of the afternoon is of the Baroque pilgrimage church of Maria Taferl, prominently positioned on the crest of a hill across the river, on a site where a number of miracles and apparitions are reputed to have taken place in the late 17th century. But the prize for the most grandiose Baroque religious confection has to go to the monastery in Melk, perched high on a granite bluff above the Danube, its mustard-yellow dome visible for several kilometres as you pedal into the town from the west. This abbey is a huge tourist magnet, and you may well find that the calming spell cast by the river is broken as you wind through the pretty but crowded streets of the Altstadt to reach your hotel.

VINE-COVERED HILLS IN THE WACHAU REGION

Day 5: Melk to Spitz
19 km (12 miles); 2 hours cycling

The abbey does not merely dominate Melk — it is Melk. You cannot leave the town without visiting it. The existing flamboyant pile was built in the first half of the 18th century, though the earlier abbey was known as a place of scholarship (and appears as such in Umberto Eco's *The Name of the Rose*) in medieval times. Highlights of a tour include the Marmorsaal (marble hall), Bibliothek (library) and Stiftskirche (abbey church). Leaving Melk, the scenery changes as you ride into the Wachau region, the most beautiful part of the trip. There is an option to leave the main route here and climb away from the river for great views to Artstetten, the home and resting place of Archduke Franz Ferdinand, whose assassination sparked the First World War. The broad plain that you have been pedalling across begins to narrow in the Wachau, as vine-covered hills gather closer to the river. The river traffic also builds up here, though in modern times the Danube plays a much less integral part in the way of life in the Wachau than it did a century ago. Riverside villages such as Spitz rely today on viticulture and tourism rather than river trade: sitting in your hotel quaffing a local vintage, you may feel that this is not altogether a bad thing.

ST STEPHEN'S CATHEDRAL, VIENNA

THE MAGNIFICENT SCHÖNBRUNN PALACE IN VIENNA IS A FINE EXAMPLE OF BAROQUE ARCHITECTURE

Day 6: Spitz to Krems
21 km (13 miles); 2 hours cycling

The villages of the Wachau become implausibly lovely this morning. Weissenkirchen is the first stop: a much-photographed, almost perfect village set among vineyards above the river. But continue along the left bank another 6 km (3¾ miles) before stopping for lunch in Dürnstein, where Richard the Lionheart was imprisoned on his way home from the Third Crusade. The afternoon drifts downhill — with the odd diversion to a vineyard for a tasting — as far as the town of Krems. Depending on how many vineyards you have stopped at, there should be plenty of time to explore the medieval centre.

Day 7: Krems to Vienna

A short train ride brings you back to Vienna, where you transfer to the elegant and delightfully old-fashioned Hotel Stefanie. The day is free to explore the Innere Stadt, or town centre: the Hofburg (a former imperial palace and now full of museums as well as the famous Spanish Riding School), the Kunsthistorisches Museum, the Stephansplatz (for Viennese street life) or a tram ride along the Ringstrasse are all tempting possibilities. And the music of Schubert, Mozart and a number of other great composers is so closely associated with Vienna that you just have to take in one of the many concerts that take place during the summer evenings.

Day 8: Departure

Transfer to the airport for the flight home.

CONTACT:
FREEWHEEL HOLIDAYS
EXECUTIVE CENTRE CARDIFF
31A CATHEDRAL ROAD
CARDIFF CF11 9HA
UK
www.freewheelholidays.com
tel: +44 (0)2920 786650

Lake District, Chile / Argentina

- Route rating: moderate
- On-road (generally tarmac with sections of dirt road)
- 9 days/8 nights
- December to March

The southern latitudes of South America — from the Fortieth Parallel down to Cape Horn — offer such an extraordinary wealth of natural wonders that it is difficult to choose any one area. For the adventurous cyclist the entire region is one big, empty, raw paradise. However, if it is sheer beauty in the landscape that you seek, there is one area that shines out above all others: the Lake District.

Split by the Andean spine of sky-piercing peaks (and the border between Chile and Argentina), the Lake District looks like the Alps on steroids: a vast area of relentlessly stupendous scenery incorporating immense lakes, forests of native trees and snow-capped peaks. This ride cuts across the top of Patagonia through the middle of the Lake District, from the western shore of Lago Llanquihue in Chile to the Argentinean town of San Martín de los Andes.

Most of the ride sweeps through a chain of national parks that have proven to be a huge draw for tourists in recent decades. But the route also follows quieter roads, sometimes straying onto dirt surfaces in order to keep away from the crowds. The riding is never technical, but there are some long days and (inevitably, given the nature of the terrain) some hills to conquer. The daily strain is more than made up for, however, by the nightly comfort: accommodation is in a string of lovely hotels ranging from hospitable hosterías to the grandiose Llao Llao hotel.

One of the highlights of the trip is, oddly, a day out of the saddle: to travel from Chile to Argentina via the Paso de Perez Rosales, you take a series of ferries and buses through the very heart of the Andes. This journey alone warrants a visit to Patagonia.

THE FLAWLESS, WHITE-CAPPED CROWN OF OSORNO VOLCANO

THE ROYAL BLUE WATERS OF LAGO NAHUEL HUAPI

Day 3: Ensenada

You have various options today. In the morning, a rafting trip that is more about experiencing the river than white-knuckle rafting sets off down the Rio Petrohué. You can hike through the glacial basin of Lago Todos los Santos, bike out to the fishing village of Ralún or indulge in the excellent facilities at the lodge.

Day 4: Yan Kee Way Lodge to Llao Llao

There is no cycling today, but this is an unforgettable journey: you go from Chile into Argentina, passing over the Continental Divide and crossing the Andes along the famous Cruce del Lagos route. The day starts with a ferry ride the length of the richly coloured waters of Lago Todos los Santos (often described as Chile's most beautiful lake) beneath the towering cone of Osorno volcano, to the tiny village of Puella. A bus then takes you over Paso de Perez Rosales, a jaw-droppingly beautiful pass beneath the mighty frontier sentinel, Mount Tronador (3,553 m/11,660 ft), and through the customs and immigration point to enter Argentina. After a brief boat trip across Lago Frías, it is back onto a bus to Puerto Blest for the final boat journey across to Puerto Pañuelo in Llao Llao. Staying in the Llao Llao hotel — a national historic landmark — is a tremendous experience. Standing on a small hill between two lakes, the hotel is surrounded by woods of cypress, coigue and arrayán, with the vast Lago Nahuel Huapi on one side and on the other a majestic row of Andean peaks.

Day 1: Puerto Varas Loop
10 km (6 miles); ½ hour cycling
The group meets in the attractive lakeside town of Puerto Varas (a major local venue for adventure sports). There is ample time to set up the bikes and for a brief safety demonstration before you set off for a short loop ride along the shore of Lago Llanquihue and into the surrounding bluish-green countryside. In the evening you head to the acclaimed Restaurant Merlín for a taste of fine regional cuisine.

Day 2: Puerto Varas to Ensenada
64 km (40 miles); 4½ hours cycling
The route on this first real day of riding follows dirt roads and tarmac around Lago Llanquihue, Chile's second-largest lake.

The scenery is stunning: across the water the flawless white-capped crown of Osorno Volcano appears to be floating on a huge barge, and to your right is Calbuco Volcano. The Spaniards found the Mapuche Indians too unruly, and many areas south of Concepción were unsafe for Europeans until the 1880s, when German immigrants moved in and started industries: there is plenty of evidence of their settlements around the lake. There are some big hills to climb, but the scenery should stir your limbs. In the afternoon you come to the edge of Vincente Pérez Rosales, the grand statesman of Chile's National Parks and then to Yan Kee Way Lodge, a timber fishing lodge in a forest of native trees only a few miles from the volcanoes.

OPPOSITE: FORESTS AND PEAKS OF THE CHILEAN LAKE DISTRICT

PETROHUÉ FALLS

Day 5: Loop via Villa Catedral
67 km (42 miles); 5 hours cycling

After a day spent travelling by boat and bus, you should be raring to get back in the saddle. The ride heads past Colonia Suiza (named after the Swiss colonists who settled here and home to an excellent pastry shop) and on up to the ski area of Villa Catedral at 2,400 m (7,874 ft). It is well worth taking the cable car from here up to the restaurant/confitería, as the panorama over the mountains and the patchwork of lakes of the entire Llao Llao region is sensational. In the evening it's time to tango — there is a dance class at the hotel.

Day 6: Llao Llao to Villa La Angostura
21 km (13 miles); 2½ hours cycling

From the hotel a ferry carries you across Lago Nahuel Huapi to the Quetrihué Peninsula in Los Arrayánes National Park. This small park and its peninsula in the lake are often overlooked by tourists. The road through the park, which was set up to protect the cinnamon-barked arrayán tree, a relative of myrtle, is quiet, and you stop for a picnic lunch on the beach. If you have had enough of pedalling in the afternoon, the lakeside resort of Villa La Angostura has plenty of shops and confiterías to amuse you. Accommodation for tonight is in the homely local hostería, Naranjo en Flor, an altogether different but cosier experience from the Llao Llao hotel.

Day 7: Villa La Angostura

The lakes and rivers of the Andes are famed for their game fishing, and today

LLAO LLAO HOTEL — AN ARGENTINEAN HISTORIC LANDMARK

is the day to test your casting skills if you wish. There is no organized ride, but those itching to get back in the saddle could try two excellent 16-km (10-mile) round trips, to the ski resort at Cerro Bayo and the Rio Bonito waterfall. Plenty of excellent hikes beckon, too; you may climb up into the hills or explore the flora along the lakeside.

Day 8: Villa La Angostura to San Martín de los Andes
115 km (72 miles); 7 hours cycling

This is the longest day of the trip by some margin. Heading north from Villa La Angostura with the mountains on your left, you ride into the Region of Seven Lakes, through impressive stands of beech. If it were possible, the scenery here is even more enthralling than it has been during the past week, as the dirt road rises over the hills and winds down between lakes Espejo, Correntoso, Hermoso and Falkner. The end of the road — no doubt a welcome sight at the end of this testing ride — is San Martín de los Andes on Lago Lácar, a town that has so far avoided the worst kind of tourism development, though it is encroaching. The Hostería La Cheminèe is situated in the centre of the town.

Day 9: San Martín de los Andes

The final day is for you to enjoy at your leisure. Those still full of running could head off on a lovely ride into the forest of Las Bandurrias National Park. Or you could try the excellent fly-fishing around the town, or succumb to shopping for local crafts in the market. In the evening the group gathers for a final dinner.

CONTACT:

BACKROADS

801 CEDAR STREET

BERKELEY, CA 94710-1800

USA

www.backroads.com

tel: +1 510 527 1555

Fernie to Akamina-Kishinena,
Rocky Mountains, Canada

- Route rating: moderate
- Off-road
- 7 days/6 nights
- Dates: July and August

The further modern life removes us from the wilderness, the more we seem to become addicted to spending time in it. This trip is for people who need a fix. Using fire trails and old logging roads, the ride explores the valleys and passes of the remote and scarcely populated south-eastern corner of British Columbia, a beautiful, quiet and unspoilt part of the planet that has changed little since the Rocky Mountains were sculpted by a succession of ice ages that began a quarter of a million years ago.

There is some human imprint on the land, of course, not least the trails you ride on — a combination of single-track, double-track and gravel forestry roads. This is an off-road trip that does not require advanced biking skills; the emphasis is not on terrifying descents that demand your full concentration (though there are a couple of these), but on having the time to look up and enjoy the fantastic scenery. You do need to be in good shape, however, as there are some hefty climbs — up to two hours — to contend with. But there is

always a van lurking nearby if you run out of steam. There are also two guides for each group (of ten) who ride with you and help set up camp. The campsites are all in superb locations, and sitting around a campfire listening to the river and counting the stars in the firmament is a highlight of the trip.

The ride starts and finishes in Fernie, a mountain town tucked away in a narrow valley in the south Canadian Rockies. Fernie had a fleeting moment of prosperity (based on coal mining, which has left a number of abandoned mines and heritage sites) at the beginning of the 20th century, but it soon drifted back into agreeable obscurity. More recently, aficionados of back-country skiing have discovered the powder bowls above the town, and their summer counterparts, the mad-boy mountain bikers, now increasingly arrive in great numbers, too. There is a large network of maintained forestry roads — perfect for mountain-biking initiates — which head up the mountainsides and give access to some challenging single-track trails that drop off into the trees.

Fernie is the kind of town where visiting outdoor enthusiasts from the big city go weak at the knees, give up their jobs and

move in, all before the weekend is over. *Outside*, an American outdoor lifestyle magazine, included it in its list of '20 Dream Towns and Adventure Hideouts'. You have been warned: you visit at your own risk.

The 170-km (106-mile) ride is spread over five days, and its goal is Akamina-Kishinena Provincial Park, a small area of reserved wilderness tucked far away from anything or anyone, on the boundary between the provinces of British Columbia and Alberta and the Canada-USA border. This wilderness area of high alpine ridges, lakes and deep valleys is contiguous with Glacier National Park, home to the last self-sustaining population of grizzly bears in the US. You will see remnants of oil rigs and mining from the 20th century, but man's involvement with this remote place goes back much further: cairns trace the paths of the Ktunaxa aboriginal people who crossed South Kootenay pass to hunt buffalo on the plains to the northeast.

Only a handful of hikers and mountain bikers make it up here every year, and if plans to create a transfrontier wildlife corridor linking Banff and Yellowstone National Parks go ahead, cycling here may be proscribed altogether — all the more reason to visit now.

HOT SINGLE-TRACK TRAILS ABOVE THE TOWN OF FERNIE

Day 1: Arrival in Fernie

The nearest international airport is Calgary. A scenic three-hour transfer through the eastern Rockies brings you to Fernie.

Day 2: Fernie
30 km (19 miles); 5 hours cycling

After breakfast at the lodge in Fernie and a session setting up and oiling the bikes, you take off for a day of warm-up rides on the extensive trail network in the mountains above Fernie — no doubt about it, this is mountain biking heaven. Spectacular views of the Elk River valley are to be had along Coal Creek Trail, which follows the old road from Fernie as far as an abandoned early 20th-century coal-mining town, through cedar forests (with some enormous trees) and stands of Douglas fir. Most of these mountain-biking routes have names. Nature Trail, Roots and the more esoteric Roots Extension should get you into the swing of things by lunchtime, when a fine picnic is laid out for you at the bottom of one of your descents. There is no set route for today: in the afternoon you can ride as much or as little as you like before dropping back down to the town for dinner at the lodge.

Day 3: Fernie to Elk River Bluffs
40 km (25 miles); 6 hours cycling

You take the River Road (they certainly don't complicate place names around here) out of Fernie as far as Silver Spring Lakes. These three crystal-clear, sparkling pools are hard to pass up, and (even better) there are cliffs for jumping off. This area is good for spotting wildlife; elk and Rocky Mountain big-horned sheep abound, and there is also a good chance of seeing moose, mule deer and white-tail deer, as well as eagles and ospreys fishing on the river. In the afternoon the fire road rolls along through fabulous scenery and old-growth cedar forests to a spectacular campsite 460 m (1,500 ft) up on sandstone bluffs overlooking the Elk River.

Day 4: Elk River Bluffs to Wigwam River
35 km (22 miles); 6 hours cycling

Today's route heads up onto and across the Wigwam Flats Wildlife Conservancy. The hour-long climb first thing in the morning brings you to a broad, dry plain covered in scrub bush and pine forests. There are superb views from here towards the mighty cliffs known as the China Wall on Mount Broadwood. There is plenty of wildlife here, too: black and grizzly bears are indigenous to this part of the Rockies, but they are very elusive. You drop off the plain and down to the Wigwam River, in an area that was inhabited by Kootenai Indians before miners came prospecting for black coal. A 5-km (3-mile) climb after lunch, followed by a 1-km (1/2-mile) single-track descent, brings you to the secluded sub-alpine Snowshoe Lake. Then it is back down to the campsite, on a gravel spit at a bend in the Wigwam River, for a solar-powered shower or a (very) brief dip in the clear, fast-running water.

CANOEING ON THE CRYSTAL-CLEAR WATER
OF SILVER SPRING LAKES

Day 5: Wigwam River to Howell River
50 km (31 miles); 6 hours cycling

The toughest ascent of the week leaves the Wigwam River this morning to climb the Cabin Road forestry trail: at 21 km (13 miles) this climb sounds like a heart-stopper, but it is a very gradual ascent and ridable all the way. From Cabin Pass there are spectacular views up to the bare, fretted mountain peaks, and you can cool off in the river before lunch. What goes up must come down, and now you reap a lovely 20-km (12½-mile) descent on a hard-packed gravel road that rolls out into the bottom of the valley. This is the longest day of the trip, and you will be happy to see the beautiful campsite at Howell Creek. Sitting round a campfire, gazing at the stars after a fine dinner, may bring out the inner-cowboy in you: a guitar is conveniently available in the back of the vehicle should you experience any such urges.

Day 6: Howell River to Fernie
25 km (16 miles); 3 hours cycling

A one-hour transfer brings you to the edge of the Akamina-Kishinena Park. Then it is onto the bikes for a slow climb — on an early 20th-century logging road that turns into single-track — up to Wall Lake, a spectacular alpine lake encircled by 600 m (2,000 ft) cliffs. Access here is on two wheels or foot only, and as few as 30 people make it up here each summer, so you are highly unlikely to have your moment at the lake ruined by hordes of tourists. Then you turn around and point your wheels back the way you came, and scream all the way down to the campsite. The bikes are loaded into the vehicles for the drive back to Fernie.

Day 7: Departure

There is time for one last, wistful walk round Fernie before transferring back to Calgary airport.

CONTACT:
FERNIE FAT-TIRE ADVENTURES
BOX 2037
FERNIE, BC V0B 1M0
CANADA
www.berniefattire.com
tel: +1 250 423 7849

RIDING ACROSS THE WIGWAM FLATS WILDLIFE CONSERVANCY

Banff to Jasper, Canada

- Route rating: moderate
- On-road
- 6 days/5 nights
- Dates: late June to August

The Canadian Rocky Mountains are a comparatively young section of the Western Cordillera, the vast band of mountain ranges that stretches from Alaska to Mexico. Beauty comes before age in this instance, however, and the sheer glory of the Rockies will leave you reeling. Mighty snow-capped, saw-toothed peaks serrate the sky above exquisitely coloured lakes, antediluvian glaciers, great rivers and meadows carpeted in wild flowers: the Rockies have got the lot.

There are many ways in which to enjoy this heart-stopping scenery: on foot, of course; from the air in a small plane; on horseback; or in a convertible car. But for me, this is the sort of massive, awe-inspiring landscape that suits one mode of travel above all others. You really have to see the Canadian Rockies from the seat of a bicycle.

The ride starts in the busy town of Banff (founded when hot springs were discovered here in the 1880s and a tourist hotspot ever since) and ends in Jasper. Winding northwest through three national parks — Banff (Canada's first, established in 1885), Yoho and Jasper — the route cherry-picks the quietest and most scenic roads, including, of course, the famous 230-km (140-mile) Icefields Parkway. Highway 93 (as it is more prosaically known), built during the Great Depression as a job-creation project, is a sheer wonder in itself as every bend and turn delivers another incredible view.

Not surprisingly, given the nature of the terrain, good opportunities abound for viewing all kinds of wildlife on this ride. Most people come here hoping to spot a bear, but though both brown and grizzly bears do inhabit the Rockies' national parks, sightings are not very common. The best time of year to see bears is around the end of June, before the snows have melted higher up and the bears have moved up the slopes. There are, however, some moose as well as plenty of elk, big-horned mountain sheep, coyotes and mountain goats to see. Ospreys and eagles often circle the skies above.

Tourism arrived here along with the Canadian Pacific Railway and the discovery of the thermal waters, over a century ago. It is a well-developed industry offering a variety of interesting accommodations, ranging on this trip from the splendour of Château Lake Louise (and the defining views from the hotel) to the rustic charm and warmth of Num-Ti-Jah, now a converted pioneers' lodge.

No one will begrudge you a little comfort or luxury in the evenings, since the days are hard work. The average altitude for the ride is 1,500 m (5,000 ft); the trend from Banff to Jasper is slightly downhill, but there is still plenty of climbing to do, with two big passes to cross. Three days have a gain of more than 700 m (2,300 ft). The views are ample reward for your labours, however, and the payback — some of the downhills are long and glorious — is sublime. There is always a support vehicle on your tail, and the route is designed to provide riders with different distance options each day.

Clear skies do predominate in July and August, but doubtful weather of some description is never far away, and good rain gear is the first thing to pack. The average daily temperature is an agreeable 18°C (64°F), but it can change fast. This is, after all, the heart of a colossal range and the 'icy crown of the continent'. If your sensibility attracts you to mountains, this ride will enchant you.

THE ICEFIELDS PARKWAY THROUGH BANFF NATIONAL PARK

THE GLACIAL, TURQUOISE WATERS OF MORAINE LAKE

Day 1: Loop along the shores of Lake Minnewanka and back to Banff
29 km (18 miles); 2 hours cycling

At the start of day one, the group gathers at Buffalo Mountain Lodge at 10.30AM for a briefing on the week ahead. Once the bikes are set up, people set off at their own pace towards Lake Minnewanka. Almost straight away there are fine views — towards Cascade Mountain and Mount Rundle — and the route passes a number of 'hoodoos', huge and magnificent-looking pedestals of rock that have been weatherbeaten into peculiar shapes.

For lunch a fine picnic spread is laid out in a spot with striking views. The ride continues along the shore of Lake Minnewanka, the largest body of water in Banff National Park, before peeling off back to Banff. This old mountain town lives mainly off tourism, but it has a small permanent population and has managed to retain much of its charm. There is time for a leisurely wander through the streets before returning to the hotel — a typical log lodge set on a hill a kilometre (½ mile) above Banff.

Day 2: Banff to Lake Louise
67 km (42 miles); 4 hours cycling

This is a rolling ride, with an uphill bias and a few longish hills, through the Bow River Valley, so named because the indigenous Cree Indians found wood here to make hunting bows. There is very little traffic on this road, and you can concentrate on spotting wildlife as you pedal: elk, coyotes and big-horned sheep all inhabit this area and there is a chance of seeing a bear. At Johnston Canyon you can dismount for a short walk up to an imposing waterfall. The final 4-km (2½-mile) stretch is steep, but the rewards are great as the ride finishes at the door of Château Lake Louise, one of the world's most renowned hotels. The original log cabin, built by the Canadian Pacific Railway in 1890, grew in time into a palatial hotel. Today it retains much of its original grandeur, yet the rooms are modern and comfortable. The hotel is very busy with tour groups during the day, but in the evening a reverential calm returns. The setting is unsurpassed, and the glass-fronted dining room will have you spooning soup absentmindedly onto your lap as you gaze at the delicate shifting hues in the fading light across the lake.

Day 3: Lake Louise to Bow Lake
82 km (51 miles); 6 hours cycling

Today is something of a walk-in geography lesson and a terrific day's cycling. It kicks off with a 10-km (6-mile) consistent climb and a 2-km (1.3-mile) descent to Moraine Lake, the glacial, turquoise waters of which are magnificently set in a giant amphitheatre below ten mountain peaks, all of them over 3,000 m (9,840 ft). A high pass brings you to the edge of the treeless alpine tundra and on to the Great Divide Road, which is closed to traffic. There is a small monument on the pass that crosses the Continental Divide – the North American watershed – and this is a good place for respite before the climbing resumes to reach Crowfoot Glacier, a fine example of how these ice rivers are formed. The afternoon is a long, rolling climb (a hefty 40 km/25 miles in total) along the Icefields Parkway to reach Bow Lake, almost the highest point of the trip. Accommodation is in Num-Ti-Jah, a converted pioneers' lodge built by the mountain guide, hunter and outfitter Jimmy Simpson on the shore of the lake. Those with energy to spare can embark on a great hike to Bow Falls, and the rest can relax amid stuffed animal heads in the lodge's library.

SAW-TOOTHED PEAKS TOWER ABOVE THE ROAD IN BRITISH COLUMBIA

Day 4: Bow Lake to Columbia Icefields Chalet
90 km (56 miles); 6 hours cycling

Bow Summit, the highest point on the Icefields Parkway at 2,068 m (6,785 ft), is the first target of the morning. From here a short walk leads to a viewing platform and one of the finest vistas in the Canadian Rockies, over Peyto Lake to the snowy peaks beyond. A long, fast downhill is next, past Waterfowl Lake and into the North Saskatchewan River Valley, where there are views of Mount Murchison. A footpath into Mistaya Canyon might tempt you off the bike before the final act of the day, a 13-km (8-mile) climb to Sunwapta Pass (2,034 m/6,673 ft): this may sound tough and there are steep sections, but it is very doable (and of course the support vehicle is ready and waiting behind you). At the top of the hill, amid the harsh landscape of Jasper National Park, stands the Columbia Icefields Chalet, which offers dazzling views of the Athabasca Glacier. Snow coach tours run from the chalet on to the glaciers; the evening, when most of the tourists have left, is a good time to go.

Day 5: Columbia Icefields Chalet to Jasper
107 km (67 miles); 7 hours cycling

A short climb after breakfast turns into a lovely 10-km (6-mile) downhill, passing the Athabasca, Dome and Stutfield glaciers, all cut with thousands of crevasses. Leaving behind the 325-sq km (125-sq mile) Columbia Icefields, the route now heads for Sunwapta Valley, where there are big-horned sheep and mountain goats to spot. This is a lovely, freewheeling spin — you lose almost 1,000 m (3,281 ft) — and a luxurious taste of cycle touring at its best. After a picnic lunch and a pause to admire the raging Athabasca Falls, there is another climb and a drop to the river that leads all the way to the Jasper Park Lodge.

Day 6: Maligne Canyon Loop
20 km (12 miles); 1½ hours cycling

Today's ride — an out and back ride to Maligne Canyon, a 50-m (160-ft) deep limestone gorge — is entirely optional, and you may prefer to mosey around the hotel, make use of some of the many facilities or go white-water rafting instead: the Class II float down the Athabasca River offers another good opportunity to spot wildlife. The bus leaves at 12 o'clock midday to arrive five hours later back in Banff, where you can ease away any aches and pains in the mineral waters.

CONTACT:

BACKROADS

801 CEDAR ST

BERKELELY, CA 94710-1800

USA

www.backroads.com

tel: +1 510 527 1555

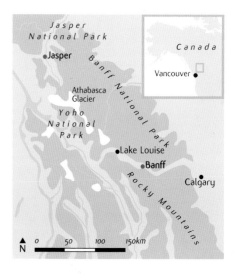

Tallinn to St Petersburg,
Estonia / Russia

- Route rating: easy
- On-road (with a few graded, un-tarmacked sections)
- 13 days/12 nights
- Dates: June to August

Estonia is not a country that swings a knockout punch to travellers. Its cultural and geographic charms, which are in fact quite substantial, seem understated, yet therein lies the key to getting the most out of this progressive Baltic state: appreciate the small, subtle details and Estonia will reveal its whole. This demands a measure of patience and sensitivity from the traveller, but in a sense this is what bicycle touring is all about: understanding by osmosis.

This 400-km (250-mile) ride – from the capital Tallinn across the flat plains and gently undulating hills of Estonia, south-east to the Russian border, round the southern edge of Lake Peipsi and then up to the magnificent city of St Petersburg – is all about learning by osmosis. There are no huge mountain ranges to cross or major festivals to attend. Rather, you pedal gently through countryside that has changed little in hundreds of years, meeting a rural people whose attachment to the land remains profound in a way that today's city dwellers struggle to understand.

There are also plenty of architectural treasures to savour on the way: in Tartu and Pechory, in Tallinn, of course (with perhaps the best-preserved medieval old town left in Europe), and most notably in St Petersburg, which needs little introduction.

The ride traverses roughly the same latitudes as Scotland, and the temperature on a summer's day can range from 20 to 30°C (68 to 86°F). It can rain a fair amount, too, but the days are long (this is the season of the fabled 'white nights' of St Petersburg), so there is always time to sit out a shower. The other type of shower might prove harder to come by, however. As anyone who has travelled cross-country in the former Soviet Union knows, the plumbing in hotels can be sketchy. Things are improving, and the hotels this trip stops at are all friendly, if a little 19th-century in their comforts. To reach the parts that other travellers cannot reach, though, you have to be prepared to take the rough with the not-so-smooth as you pedal.

THE MEDIEVAL HEART OF TALLINN

Day 1: Arrival in Tallinn
You fly to Tallinn (usually via Copenhagen) and transfer to your hotel on the edge of the small central district.

Day 2: Tallinn
The day is free to explore Tallinn. A good way to start is with a walk to the top of Toompea, the hill that dominates the heart of the city, from which there are fine views of the long city wall and the spires, pastel-coloured wooden buildings and cobbled streets of the old town, with the Baltic Sea beyond. There can be few places where the architecture and atmosphere of medieval Europe have survived as well as in Tallinn. It is a delight to wander through its jumble of lanes, steeples, courtyards, turrets, merchant houses and churches. But this is not to imply that Tallinn is hopelessly old-fashioned: on the contrary, it is a prosperous city that has completely transformed itself since Estonia became independent in 1991. Many museums have been restored, and a wealth of restaurants offer excellent, hearty Estonian cuisine. Tallinn has long been famous for its cafés, and this is definitely a place where you can have your cake and eat it as well.

Day 3: Tallinn to Kehtna
70 km (44 miles); 4½ hours cycling
The old town of Tallinn can give the impression that the Estonian economy is flourishing. But in fact the country's wealth is heavily concentrated here, and the city suburbs you pedal through this

morning tell a different story. Once in the countryside, you point your wheels southeast – the bearing you follow all the way to the Russian border south of Lake Peipsi – and pray for a following wind (the chances of which are in your favour). The route crosses the clear, slow-flowing waters of the River Keila to reach Rapla, an elegant town with a twin-towered church. A shorter leg in the afternoon brings you to Kehtna, where accommodation is in a small hotel.

Day 4: Kehtna to Poltsamaa
75 km (47 miles); 4½ hours cycling
This long day takes you past a number of manor houses and small castles, legacies of the time when the region was subdivided by a feudal aristocracy and control of the Baltic Coast was fought over by the Danish, Swedish, Russian and German armies. There is one 15-km (9-mile) stretch of unpaved road. The day's goal is Poltsamaa, a stronghold of the knights of the Teutonic Order from the 13th century, with a castle rebuilt in the decorative, Rococo style of the 18th century that was to prove an inspiration for castles all over Europe.

Day 5: Poltsamaa to Aksi
65 km (40 miles); 4 hours cycling
The countryside between Tallinn and Tartu is predominantly flat, and the cycling, often following well-signed bicycle routes down quiet roads, is correspondingly gentle. You will see the odd modern tractor, but generally the farm buildings and the machinery date from a previous

century. This is a poor part of the country, yet to be reached by the economic benefits of foreign investment and development initiatives. But the people are helpful and hospitable. The ride today brings you to the small town of Aksi, in order to set up a short ride for the morning.

Day 6: Aksi to Tartu
20 km (12 miles); 1½ hours cycling

You breeze into Estonia's second-largest city, Tartu, at mid-morning. This university town was the centre of the country's 19th-century national revival, and it retains a uniquely Estonian flavour. As a trade bridge between the Hanseatic League in the west and the rich Russian cities of Pskov and Novgorod, Tartu flourished. A great fire destroyed much of the town in the 18th century, and more recently it was devastated by both the Soviets and the Germans in the Second World War. Many of the classical buildings that remain standing today have an air of austerity about them, but the student population gives the town a youthful spirit. The rest of the day is free to explore Raejoka Plats (the cobbled main square), the university, Cathedral Hill, some excellent museums and the numerous restaurant-lined lanes that run off the main boulevards.

WINDMILLS IN THE RURAL SOUTHEAST CORNER OF ESTONIA

Day 7: Tartu to Ryapina
75 km (47 miles); 5 hours cycling

Few travellers make it as far as the lovely, rolling countryside of Setumaa, the (politically unrecognized) region southeast of Tartu. Their loss is your gain, as there is an interesting mix of cultures here: Estonians rub shoulders with Russian Old Believers (Orthodox Christians who speak a different language) and Setus, a separate ethnic group who have straddled the Russian border for generations and have given the area its name. The Setus live in villages shaped like fortified castles, with clustered houses facing inwards; since the border with Russia was created in 1991, however, the dwindling community has been divided, and Setu culture is slowly and sadly disappearing. Today's undulating route heads past Lakes Peipsi and Vortsyarv to reach the small town of Ryapina. Accommodation is in a small, welcoming hotel in the town.

Day 8: Ryapina to Pechory
35 km (22 miles); 2 hours cycling

The short morning ride brings you to the frontier with Russia. This is one of those remote border crossings (into a country that was closed for so long) that give even the hardiest travellers a frisson of excitement. Once the formalities are completed, there is time to explore Pechory, the 'capital' of Setumaa, famed for its 15th-century Orthodox monastery, one of the most extraordinary in the whole of Russia. The monks will take you on a tour.

Day 9: Pechory to Pskov
55 km (34 miles); 3 hours cycling

The Russian countryside looks tired and worn in contrast to Estonia. This is real border country and the realm of brigands, as the 13th-century fortress in Izborsk attests. In the afternoon you reach the town of Pskov, the western frontier of ancient Russia. The 20th century was not kind to Pskov, but it is still a pretty town with a lovely riverside kremlin and a number of architecturally distinctive churches.

Day 10: Pskov to St Petersburg

After the quiet country roads of rural Estonia the busy highways of Russia have little to recommend them, so you leap aboard the support vehicle for the three-hour transfer to St Petersburg. A stop on the way in the town of Pushkin (named after the poet who was educated here) allows you to admire the beautiful palaces and parks created by the Empresses Elizabeth and Catherine the Great in the second half of the 18th century.

Days 11 & 12: St Petersburg

Your hotel is just off Nevsky Prospekt, the most famous street in Russia and the perfect base for exploring. An organized tour on the first day takes in some of the main sites (Palace Square, Mars Field, Summer Gardens, the River Neva) and a canal cruise. Having found your bearings (not easy in a city this size, criss-crossed by remarkably similar canals), you are free to sightsee on your own on the second day.

Day 13: Departure

There is time for some last-minute shopping on Nevsky Prospekt before the 20-minute transfer to the airport for the flight home.

CONTACT:
EXODUS TRAVELS
GRANGE MILLS
WEIR ROAD
LONDON SW12 0NE
UK
www.exodus.co.uk
tel: +44 (0)870 240 5550

CHURCH OF THE RESURRECTION OF CHRIST, ST PETERSBURG

Mont Ventoux, France

- Route rating: strenuous
- On-road
- 6 days/5 nights
- Dates: May to June and September to October

What is the most famous cycle race of them all? The Tour de France, of course. And what is the most renowned stage of the Tour de France? The stage that goes over the top of Mont Ventoux, the legendary giant of Provence.

At 1,909 m (5,727 ft), Mont Ventoux is certainly not the highest mountain, yet its reputation goes before it by an awfully long way. The intensity of the climb, the bleak terrain at the summit and the harsh weather conditions that often prevail have ensured it a place of its own in the pantheon of great mountain climbs. Mont Ventoux's position in Tour folklore also ensures that hundreds of amateur cyclists flock to Provence every year to ride in the tracks of their heroes and — they hope — to conquer it.

Many fail, for this is a merciless mountain. Most heroically, the British cyclist Tommy Simpson rode himself to exhaustion, collapsed and died here, 1.5 km (1 mile) from the top, during the 1967 Tour de France. A granite memorial stands at the roadside to commemorate him and remind all who follow him up.

This six-day tour aims to put fit and determined cyclists safely on top. Starting from the tour base in the village of Bédoin at the foot of the mountain, a series of self-guided day-long rides take you through the hilly countryside of the Vaucluse region. They include two attempts to climb Ventoux, on days three and five, from the southwest and up the slightly easier route on the northern flank.

With its abundance of sunshine and Mediterranean climate, Provence is a holiday destination all year round. Summers can be dry and roasting hot, however, while the infamous mistral wind (Mont Ventoux is known as 'windy mountain') blows hardest in winter (and blow it does: some of the highest wind speeds ever have been recorded here). This, then, is a trip for spring or autumn, and even then the weather on top of the mountain can be cruel. Temperatures are typically 10°C (18°F) lower at the summit than down below, so a windproof jacket and arm warmers are essential gear.

All the roads on this trip are 'D' or *départementale* roads: smooth, well-maintained and used mainly by cyclists and tourists. The nature of the terrain dictates that cars cannot travel too fast.

This trip is not solely about grinding it out on the mountain, however. The Vaucluse is a beautiful region, alternately wild and gentle, heavily cultivated and uncultivable, profuse and sparse, all of which serves to make it as intriguing as its famous mountain.

Geologically, the Vaucluse is a large limestone plateau, underlaid with a complex system of subterranean rivers. Many of its towns — with their plane trees, fountains and rotund men playing boules in the lambent evening light — retain an air of charm and authenticity: it takes considerable strength of mind to pedal straight through them and not stop for a cool beer and a chat. The dry-stone villages, often perched on rocky hills, are somnolent, and the countryside, dotted with terraced fields of lavender and thyme, olive groves, peach orchards and vineyards, adds up to a bucolic vision of unspoilt rural France.

This being Provence, the eating and drinking is top-notch. Wines abound, from front-row reds such as Châteauneuf-du-Pape, Vacqueyras and Gigondas, to eminently quaffable table rosés and fortified sweet wines. The local produce, which includes renowned olive oils, cheeses, strawberries, black truffles and honey, forms the basis of a culture of serious gastronomy. There are many excellent restaurants — and once you have conquered the giant of Provence, it would be churlish not to spoil yourself.

RICH COLOURS OF THE PROVENCAL COUNTRYSIDE

Day 1: Arrival at Bédoin

Arrive at the TGV railway station in Avignon and transfer (40 km/25 miles) to the hotel in Bédoin, a pretty village at the foot of Mont Ventoux and your base for the week. Bédoin is famous for its AOC wine, a variety of fruits and asparagus. An evening aperitif comes complete with a briefing about the week ahead. If you are renting a bike, it will be fitted this evening.

Day 2: Cols and Gorges
70 km (44 miles); 3–4 hours cycling

'Cols', or mountain tops, abound in every direction and on every day of this trip, which means there are plenty of fast descents, and it is essential to check over your bike, and specifically the brakes and wheels, each morning. Today's ride is a warm-up which takes you via Combe de l'Hermitage (449 m/1,347 ft) to the top of Col des Abeilles: at 996 m (2,988 ft), this is a good initiation to climbing in Provence. The route drops down to a plateau and the beautifully situated medieval town of Sault, which offers plenty of good restaurants, a fine 13th-century church and a Gallo-Roman museum (Provence was an important province of ancient Rome), to detain you over lunch. In the afternoon, you ride down the spectacular Nesque gorge back to Bédoin.

Day 3: Ascent of Mont Ventoux
42 km (26 miles); 3–4 hours cycling

And so to climb the great mountain. It is best to start early in the morning in order both to avoid the hottest part of the day and to enjoy the views from the top, which can be affected by cloud and haze in the afternoons. This ascent is up the southwest slope from Bédoin: the most difficult route and the one taken by the Tour de France. The climb covers 21 km (13 miles), with a height gain of 1,600 m (4,800 ft). It starts easily enough, sauntering through olive groves and orchards on gradients of between two and six percent as far as the village of St Estève. On the next killer section to Chalet Renard, the gradient rises to a fearsome 11 percent in places. You will find that the shade provided by forests of cedar, beech and larch is very welcome. After Chalet Renard, you enter the idiosyncratic and bleak terrain for which Mont Ventoux is famous: a steep stone desert that provides little encouragement for aching limbs and absolutely no shelter from the wind. You pass the memorial to Tommy Simpson, strewn with dried flowers offered by passing fans, and then you are on top. It is not a prepossessing summit, studded as it is with weather and communication stations, but you are now a vertical mile above the plains of Provence, and on a clear day the views are outstanding, encompassing the Alps, the Rhône Valley and the entire Vaucluse plateau. Soak them in at the top, because on the way down you will want to concentrate on one thing alone — the road. The descent all the way back to Bédoin is very fast.

Day 4: Rest day
This is scheduled as a rest day, and there is certainly much to encourage you away from your bike; the 12th-century Cistercian abbey at Sénanque, the Renaissance château at Gordes and the amazing ochre quarries around Roussillon are three highlights of the area. They can easily be combined to make a bike tour, or for those looking for something tougher, the trip organizers can propose a long circuit around the Vaucluse that crosses no fewer than 20 cols.

THE BLEAK SUMMIT OF MONT VENTOUX

Mont Ventoux, France

Day 5: Ascent of Mont Ventoux
66 km (42 miles); 4 hours cycling

Today's ascent follows the northern route up the mountain. This is marginally easier than the road from Bédoin (at least there is nothing as gruelling as the section through the forest above St Estève). A pleasant warm-up brings you after 12 km (7½ miles) to the village of Malaucaine, where the climb begins. Because of the terracing of the land there are short sections of respite on this road, but don't be fooled: this is still Mont Ventoux. From Malaucaine to the summit is 21 km (13 miles). There is a place to stop for a drink at Chalet Liotard, and then it is the lonely road to the summit. Unnervingly, the top is visible when you are still a long way from it, but when you hit the chalk road markings and graffiti your goal is near. Another fast free-wheel will return you swiftly to Malaucaine for a celebratory lunch.

Day 6: Departure

Pack up (or return) your bikes and transfer back to Avignon railway station.

CONTACT:
CYCLING CLASSICS
8630 E. VIA DE VENTURA 110
SCOTTSDALE, AZ 85258
USA
www.cyclingclassics.com
tel: +1 800 960 2221

Loire Valley, France

- Route rating: easy
- On-road
- 6 days/5 nights
- Dates: April to October

The Loire Valley is quintessentially French: the lush countryside alone, cut by wide, languid rivers with banks of reeds and willows, will be enough to set the hearts of Francophiles racing. Add to this the superb cuisine, the delicate white wines, the heady scent of flowers, the profusion of ornate Renaissance châteaux and, reputedly, the purest French accent of all, and you begin to appreciate why the region is known as the 'heart of France'.

With its wealth of attractions and its proximity to Paris, it is not surprising that the Loire became a battleground between French and foreign protagonists. In the 15th century the English under Henry V controlled all of France north of the river, and Joan of Arc famously raised the siege of Orléans, a reversal of French fortunes that tipped the scales and saw the English driven from the Continent. With the French ascendancy the Loire entered its heyday, earning the soubriquet 'Valley of the Kings': throughout much of the Renaissance this lovely valley became the backdrop to French courtly life, aristocratic intrigues and architectural excess.

The legacy of all this is a remarkable collection of fairytale châteaux, a number of which are on the route and one of which is now a hotel where you spend the first two nights. Many of these châteaux are built of tufa, the porous rock that you see along the river. A remarkable feature of this pale stone is that it bleaches with the passage of time, ensuring that, under their jet-black slate roofs, the châteaux still look brand new. A variety of museums (including one devoted to Leonardo da Vinci, who spent the last few years of his life here) and lively markets in the bustling towns along the river will also vie with each other to tempt you out of the saddle.

Needless to say, the Loire Valley is something of a tourist honey-pot, with coaches and air-conditioned cars jamming main roads and the car parks of major sites in the height of summer. On two wheels, however, you can mosey along quiet lanes and back roads, past vineyards and farms, avoiding the worst of the overheated kerfuffle.

There are different distance options for each day on this tour, so you only have to pedal as far as you wish. Yet the cycling is never anything but easy. The menus you will be presented with at the end of each day provide a more substantial challenge, however. In the aristocratic heyday of the valley, gargantuan feasts were the norm, and food remains a matter of the highest importance in the Loire today. This trip takes in Michelin-starred restaurants and châteaux dining rooms, so even if you leave your cycling legs at home, be sure to bring a large appetite.

ELEGANT GARDENS AT CHENONCEAU

Day 1: Montbazon Loop
15 km (9 miles); 1 hour cycling

A 30-minute transfer brings you from the meeting point at the main railway station in Tours, with its Gothic town centre, to the Château d'Artigny. This magnificent château perched high above the Indre (a major tributary of the Loire) was renovated in extravagant fashion by the famous perfumer François Coty. It is now a lavish hotel and your base for the first two nights of this trip. On your arrival the group leader will help fit you to your bike, and after a brief talk you head off on a warm-up ride. The great novelist Honoré de Balzac lived in the Indre Valley for many years, and the landscape and river, which he described as 'unravelling like a serpent in a magnificent emerald basin', featured in many of his works. The short ride through forests, sunflower fields and quiet villages is a gentle appetizer for the days ahead. Back at the Château d'Artigny there is plenty to explore, from the kitchen and wine cellars (a guided tour with the hotel's sommelier) to the spacious lawns and terraces overlooking the valley. Dinner — the first of many fine feasts this week — takes place in Coty's sumptuous dining room.

Day 2: Villandry Loop
57 km (35 miles); 4 hours cycling

The famed vineyards of the Loire line the road along the River Indre to Azay-le-Rideau, the setting for one of France's most architecturally perfect châteaux. This small but exquisitely proportioned early Renaissance building reflects the architectural shift in the 16th century from defensive castles to pleasure palaces of the aristocracy. It still boasts turrets and a moat, but its battlements are ornamental. After lunch the route heads north, away from the Indre and across Touraine towards the River Cher and the small town of Villandry. The château here is famous for its gardens, restored to Renaissance grandeur at the beginning of the 20th century. Here you wander down through three stunning tiers of gardens — water, ornamental and kitchen — and into a world reminiscent of *Alice in Wonderland*.

Day 3: Montbazon to Amboise
69 km (43 miles); 5 hours cycling

The route heads east today, through forests and across a landscape that has changed little since counts and courtiers built their palaces here in order to be close to the court of the king. The pedalling, like the country, is gentle, as you pass through Cormery to reach the Château de Nitray for lunch and a wine tasting. In the afternoon the River Cher leads you to the most famous of the Loire Valley châteaux, Chenonceau, the elegant arches of which span the river. Catherine de Medici, wife of Henry II, and Diane de Poitiers, his mistress, were among the powerful women who perfected this exquisite château. A guided tour takes you around the elaborate interior and explains the château's fascinating history, and then you can explore the gardens on your own. The last few kilometres head across open countryside to the banks of the Loire and Amboise, a lively provincial French town with a colourful street market full of vendors selling the excellent produce of the region. Accommodation is at Le Choiseul, a converted 18th-century manor house with a Michelin-starred restaurant, so there is good reason to get excited about dinner.

Day 4: Seillac Loop
63 km (39 miles); 5 hours cycling

You have to climb out of Amboise, following the Loire upstream, to reach the hilltop castle of Chaumont. Here, as in so many of the châteaux in the region, the political intrigues, plots and shenanigans of the Renaissance French court were played out in fabulous surroundings (albeit often brutally, as attested by the display of arms in the Salle des Gardes). With its round towers and expansive lawns above the river, Chaumont is both picturesque and impressive. There is time for a tour of the château's interior before lunch. Today you are free to have a picnic in the surrounding parkland or try out some local dishes in a restaurant in Chaumont. In the afternoon the route continues through the countryside on the other side of the Loire, as far as the village of Seillac before you swing round and head back to Amboise. You should be back in time to wander the lovely streets and explore the 15th-century château that once housed the court of the French king. Largely demolished during the Revolution, the château nevertheless retains some outstanding features, including the beautiful Chapelle St Hubert.

CHÂTEAU D'AZAY-LE-RIDEAU, A TREASURE OF EARLY RENAISSANCE FRENCH ARCHITECTURE

RIGHT: PEDALLING THROUGH FIELDS OF SUNFLOWERS

OPPOSITE: THE VILLAGE OF GARGILESSE IN THE 'VALLEY OF THE KINGS'

Day 5: Amboise to Les Hautes Roches
51 km (32 miles); 4 hours cycling

The ride barely gets rolling this morning before reaching the first stop at the château of Le Clos Lucé, the final resting place of Leonardo da Vinci. Patronized by François I, da Vinci spent the last years of his life here (becoming fascinated by the soft light of the Loire Valley), and the charming old building is now a museum housing models of many of his masterful, futuristic inventions. Then you are bowling across the distinctive, vineyard-covered countryside of the region, past some well-preserved Troglodyte dwellings (there are many along the Loire), towards the village of Vouvray, famed for its Chenin Blanc vineyards. You can learn about the interesting history of this wine region (the wines of Vouvray were already popular in the 8th century, and more recently the TGV train line was sent underground to avoid digging up the vineyards) on a private guided tour of a cave with a local winemaker. After a picnic lunch (and possibly a siesta), it is back on the saddle through the famed Vouvray vineyards past Chateau de Valmer to Rochecorbon and Les Hautes Roches, a delightful hotel beside the river with another Michelin-starred restaurant, where the final session of fine dining takes place.

Day 6: Les Hautes Roches to Tours
18 km (11 miles) 1½ hours cycling

There is a short spin this morning (not least to work off a little of the gastronomic indulgence) as far as La Grange de Meslay, a medieval fortified farm, before packing up and transferring (30 minutes) to the main railway station in Tours. Paris is one to three hours away depending on which train you take.

CONTACT:
BACKROADS
801 CEDAR STREET
BERKELEY, CA 94710-1800
USA
www.backroads.com
tel: +1 510 527 1555

Pyrenees, France / Spain

- Route rating: strenuous
- Off-road (predominantly single-track)
- 8 days/7 nights
- Dates: May to September

Bagnères de Luchon, high in the central Pyrenees, owes its place on the map to its therapeutic spring waters. The Romans first dug out hot spa pools here, and major investment in the 18th century drew the French aristocracy in sufficient numbers for the town to be popularly renamed the 'Queen of the Pyrenees'. Luchon — the familiar abbreviation — still attracts thousands of visitors every year, looking for relaxing treatments and soothing massages.

Mountain bikers, however, come here for a fix of a very different kind. Luchon, midway between the Atlantic Ocean and the Mediterranean in the Hautes Pyrénées, is tucked in beneath the 15 highest peaks of the entire 400-km (250-mile) range. It is the gateway to one of Europe's classic mountain biking areas, offering an inexhaustible choice of exhilarating downhill riding (as well as a cable car to lift you back up). If you want vertical descent, then Luchon is for you. This is hammerhead heaven.

The routes — on mountain footpaths, old shepherds' roads and forest trails — lead up the Luchon Valley, across to the neighbouring Vallée d'Oueil and over the border into the Val d'Aran in Spain, where the River Garonne begins its long journey to Bordeaux and the Bay of Biscay. This is the highest, most remote part of the Pyrenees, accessible only to hikers and serious mountain bikers: an area of dramatic rugged countryside with an array of interesting fauna. You are unlikely to spot a lynx or a bear, though they do inhabit the Haute Garonne, but wild boar, izard and roe deer abound. The area is also home to eagles, red kites and the endangered bearded vulture, Europe's largest bird of prey — a fantastic sight, if you are lucky enough to see it wheeling above the granite cliffs on stiff wings. The base for the week is La Fenière, a

comfortable and remote private mountain lodge in the Vallée du Lys, a few miles from Luchon. The stone building is a converted barn in a wonderful setting. The bedrooms are simple, but there is a grand living room and a large garden with views of the mountains where you can lounge at the end of each day. Nearby on the River Lys is a deep pool for swimming. Meals (except one dinner) are all prepared at the lodge.

The day rides usually start with a vehicle transfer (to gain some extra height), followed by a gentle warm-up climb, and finish at a bar in the town for an apéritif. The great majority of the exhilarating trails are single-track, and you do need a good machine for this (mountain bikes can be hired). The bias is towards descent, but there is no avoiding at least a little climbing (typically 100–400 m, or up to a quarter of a mile, of vertical gain per day), some of which is tough: a good level of fitness helps. The rides are all led by an experienced mountain-biking guide, who knows these routes well and can help you improve your technique. Most of the tougher sections are optional, allowing skilled, fit riders to test the outer limits of their abilities, while everyone else can progress evenly, taking on greater challenges as the week goes by. However, you do need to come with a strong will to ride, and to ride hard.

LOOKING OVER A FIELD OF BUTTERCUPS

TOWARDS THE HIGH PEAKS OF THE PYRENEES

Day 1: Arrival at La Fenière

You will be met off your flight at Toulouse airport for the two-and-a-half-hour transfer to the Luchon Valley. The evening is spent preparing bikes and settling in at La Fenière, your base for the whole week.

Day 2: La Fenière to Luchon, via Les Ruines d'Herran and Artigue
35 km (22 miles); 6 hours cycling

This gentle warm-up day starts at Les Ruines d'Herran, overlooking the Luchon Valley (a 45-minute vehicle transfer from the lodge), and follows the contours on wide tracks to the village of Artigue. At this altitude beech and pine predominate. Much of the morning's ride is through cool forests with spectacular views over the foothills of the Pyrenees. The first section of single-track starts at Gouaux-de-Luchon. It is neither technical nor steep — a perfect introduction for initiates to the mountain-biking nirvana — but there is plenty of it: a total of 1,700 m (1 mile) in descent today. There are short road interludes to link up the trails along the valley floor that end up back in Luchon, at one of the many bars in this pretty town.

CLASSIC SINGLETRACK TRAILS IN THE PYRENEES

Day 3: Vallée d'Oueil
45 km (28 miles); 5½ hours cycling

A 30-minute transfer delivers you to the Vallée d'Oueil, where the main ascent of the day starts: a gradual climb on a lane, through quiet villages, up this beautiful valley. At the top ridge you are rewarded with extensive views of the mountains. Take time to savour these wonderful sights, because you will not want to be distracted on the way down — a fast, exciting descent which finishes in the village of Bourg d'Oueil. Dotted about the hillsides are a number of Bronze Age burial cairns. There is more single-track en route to the next village, Benqué, where you can take a short break and discover the pretty late medieval church. From here the group can split (as with many of the rides, the most demanding and technical sections of single-track can be avoided if you prefer); experienced riders can really test themselves, while the merely mortal and the sane can mosey gently back along the road to Luchon. That bar on your return will be a welcome sight; this is a tougher day, with 1,400 m (4,590 ft) of climbing.

REMOTE COUNTRYSIDE IN THE HAUTE PYRÉNÉES

Day 4: La Carrière to Luchon, via Oo
50 km (31 miles); 6½ hours cycling

There is more descent than ascent on every day of this week, but the fit and youthful can choose to start today with a climb up to La Carrière to meet the rest of the group in the vehicle. Then it is on to a lovely track, contouring through the forests of the Luchon Valley again, before a stiff, short climb to the hamlet of Granges de Labach. The next section of single-track is a real shakedown: a 50-minute descent on a path with rough sections and covered in roots. (There is an alternative route down.) This is real mountain biking and strictly for the headstrong. Obviously you need a good-quality mountain bike, preferably with discbrakes. Lunch is a picnic beside the river in the village of Oo, followed by more hot trails that bring you, once again, back to Luchon.

Day 5: Free day

There is no guided ride today, but there is still plenty of cycling to be done, on fresh trails or on road, over one of the famous Tour de France cols such as the Portillon or the Peyresourde. Road bikes are available for hire in Luchon. The Hautes Pyrénées is a multi-activity area and you can try your hand at tandem paragliding, kayaking, white-water rafting, canyoning and more. Or you may prefer to lie in the sun or avail yourself of some pampering at the baths in Luchon. Dinner is not provided at the lodge tonight, but Luchon offers a number of acclaimed restaurants.

OPPOSITE: THE ANTENAC RIDGE, ABOVE LUCHON

Day 6: Superbagnères ski station
65 km (40 miles); 7 hours cycling

This is the big day of descent: a full-on seven-hour session at the Superbagnères ski resort, plunging from 1,800 m (5,900 ft) down to Luchon at 600 m (1,960 ft) in order to catch the *télécabine* back up. It is possible to do this four times in a day – effectively a cool 5 km (3 miles) of descent – or more if you are very fit. The classic, the Vallée Blanche of Pyrenean mountain biking, is the run from Techous to Castel Vieih, dropping 900 m (nearly 3,000 ft) through woodland on switchback trails. In the right mood and on the right day, you might just reach oneness with your wheels on this descent. There are many different routes, however, of varying grades, making this a very good opportunity for everyone to improve their mountain-biking skills.

Day 7: Val d'Aran
55 km (34 miles); 7 hours cycling

The great mountain chain of the Pyrenees, which stretches from the Atlantic to the Mediterranean, is broken in only one place: at Val d'Aran, a high valley that bisects the central massif, where the River Garonne rises. The last day is spent exploring here. It takes an hour in the vehicle to get over the border into Spain and the start of the ride. There are a number of rides in this valley – some harder than others – and the guide will advise you. Much of the climbing, which can be tough, is on fire trails and the descents on single-track: the perfect combination. The panoramic views,

especially from Col de Varrados and Col de Pruedo, over alpine meadows towards the highest peaks in the Pyrenees – Aneto (3,404 m/11,167 ft) and Posets (3,375 m/11,073 ft) – are remarkable. It is possible to ride all the way down, back to the lodge, for a final night of fine French *paysan* food.

Day 8: Departure

Pack the bikes up and transfer to Toulouse airport.

CONTACT:
EXODUS TRAVELS
GRANGE MILLS
WEIR ROAD
LONDON SW12 0NE
UK
www.exodus.co.uk
tel: +44 (0)870 240 5550

Antigua to Lanquín, Guatemala

- Route rating: strenuous
- Off-road (with a few short sections of tarmac)
- 17 days/16 nights
- Dates: November to late February

Guatemala might just be the most colourful country on the planet. Nature's paintbox here encompasses white and black sands, red lava, a thousand shades of forest green, umber soil and the fabulous burnished orange of the beautiful sunsets. Then there are the rainbow-coloured traditional costumes of the Mayan people, the pastels of Antigua's colonial buildings and the vibrant pigments of the local textiles.

This quite extraordinary palette of chromatic action, however, may pass you by in one furious technicolor blur, as this particular trip is about serious mountain biking and not for the faint-hearted: from single-track descents of the volcanoes above Antigua to back-country trails in the Cuchumatanes Mountains, these are 14 days of hell-for-leather riding. You have to be bang up for it and fully prepared, even if it does mean seeing Guatemala in one long, bright shimmer of colour.

The trip starts and finishes in Antigua, the former imperial capital of Central and South America. The Spanish Conquistadors built the city, setting it regally below a trio of volcanoes. Despite three major earthquakes, many of the colonial buildings still stand, albeit now gracefully ruined. This is also the cultural and party capital of Guatemala, and the perfect place both to introduce yourself to the country and to end your trip with a bang.

The ride also takes in Guatemala's other main traveller attraction, Lake Atitlán. After this, however, you leave the tourists behind for an off-road adventure in the wilds of the Cuchumatanes Mountains. This is an area still scarred by Guatemala's brutal civil war, which dragged on until 1996, and little exposed to tourism, but the people – in their fabulous finery – are bright and friendly. The finale is a visit to the natural wonder of Semuc Champey.

SAWDUST PAINTINGS ON THE STREETS OF ANTIGUA

Day 1: Arrival in Antigua

Arrive in Guatemala City and transfer (45 minutes) to the hotel in Antigua.

Day 2: Loop through the Valley of Antigua
24 km (15 miles); 2½ hours cycling

After a morning assembling bikes and ambling through the cobbled streets comes a warm-up ride into the countryside surrounding the city.

Day 3: Loop onto the slopes of Agua volcano
26 km (16 miles); 3 hours cycling

Antigua is magnificently situated beneath three hanging volcanoes (one of which occasionally spouts a column of ash as a reminder of its potency), and today's ride is a classic mountain-bike route up Agua volcano (3,766 m/12,360 ft). Following quiet roads and jeep tracks, you reach the higher slopes and the views: seize these and catch your breath, because the ride down is a screamer, on single-track through coffee plantations to hit the valley floor 700 m (half a mile) below. Then it's back into the city for a night on the town. Antigua is a major party capital, with endless bars and clubs that rock until dawn.

Day 4: Antigua to Lake Atitlán
51 km (32 miles); 5 hours cycling

The day starts with a 90-minute transfer (along the Pan-American Highway) towards the Western Highlands and the well-maintained Mayan ruins at Ixmiché. This is fertile, cultivated and beautiful countryside dotted with farmers' settlements and pine forests. The ride, on dirt roads with sections of single-track, leads dramatically to the edge of the caldera surrounding Lake Atitlán, which Aldous Huxley famously described as 'the most beautiful lake in the world'. It is wondrously set in a huge crater that links three further volcanoes. The single-track from the rim down to the lakeside village of Santa Catarina Palopo is one of the best rides of the trip. A short boat ride brings you to the La Casa del Mundo hotel, set atmospherically on a cliff overlooking the lake. Needless to say, this is a good spot for a well-earned beer.

Day 5: Lake Atitlán to Santiago
29 km (18 miles); 3 hours cycling

Another boat shuttle brings you to San Marco la Laguna, a small town set on a promontory, where the lakeside trail begins. The surface is rough until you pick up the dirt road that leads round the back of San Pedro volcano. A switchback ascent threads between the many peaks on the southwest side of the lake before the route drops back down through vast coffee plantations to Santiago. This fascinating town has a strong tradition of making the beautiful embroidered clothing for which Guatemala is renowned. It is also known for its strange blend of evangelical, Roman Catholic and idol worship, which throws up some very strange festivals around Easter. Accommodation is in the Posada de Santiago, a lovely hotel set in its own gardens, with a highly reputed restaurant.

Day 6: Santiago to Huehuetenango

In a sense this trip divides in two: the first half, in Antigua and around Lake Atitlán, is firmly on the Guatemalan tourist trail, and you will see travellers, holistic centres, language schools and backpackers galore. The second half heads off into the remote Cuchumatanes Mountains, the largest area over 3,000 m (9,800 ft) high in Central America and a region that was thick with guerrilla activity during the civil war. The terrain prevented government forces from quelling the area completely, and travellers have only gradually returned after the 1996 ceasefire. The region remains remote and is very hilly, but then that's precisely why you bring a mountain bike here. No cycling today — it is a six-hour bus journey to Huehuetenango, the busy regional capital, where you will have time in the afternoon to visit the market to buy whatever you need for the days ahead.

Day 7: Huehuetenango to Todos Santos
46 km (29 miles); 6 hours cycling

A short distance from Huehuetenango the ride kicks off for real, with a 1 km (just over half a mile) climb on tarmac to reach a 3,300 m (10,830 ft) pass from which the views are astonishing: you feel you can see most of Central America. You cross an arid plateau on tarmac before a section of dirt road leads up to the beginning of a long and fast descent into the town of Todos Santos. Clouds often sink among these mountains in the late afternoon, so you may descend through the mists. Todos Santos is a remote town inhabited

MAYAN RUINS

by indigenous people, superstitious and sometimes shy. Costumes are traditional and striking, the language is Mam, and adherence to an unchanged way of life is strong. But the Todos Santeros are friendly (and their festivals are insane). The town — effectively one street squeezed into a valley hemmed in by 3,800 m (12,470 ft) mountains — is a riot of colour.

Day 8: Todos Santos to the Blue Unicorn
40 km (25 miles); 4 hours' cycling

There is time to explore Todos Santos in the morning before heading off towards the Ixil village of Nebaj. The landscape is a mix of pine and coniferous forests, bare peaks and fertile valley floors. The Blue Unicorn Hotel stands on the main ridge of the Cuchumatanes Mountains, overlooking Huehuetenango and with sweeping panoramas of the south.

Day 9: The Blue Unicorn to Aguacatán
45 km (28 miles); 6 hours' cycling

After a few days of hauling uphill, today's ride swings the other way with a descent of 1,300 m (4,270 ft). The route drops off the southern end of the Cuchumatanes Mountains, following switchback dirt roads or, for the headstrong and brave, horse tracks that take a more direct route to the valley below. The final 20-km (12½-mile) stretch follows the river — you are in the warmer lowlands now — to the market town of Aguacatán, where you'll see the women are as elaborately dressed as anywhere in Guatemala. This is the home of outstanding coffee which is worth sampling. Accommodation is in a family-run hostel where the local food is excellent.

Day 10: Aguacatán to Nebaj
62 km (39 miles); 8 hours cycling

This is a gruelling day, with 1,855 m (over a mile) of climbing. There is also plenty of downhill and superb scenery, but it is still the toughest day of the trip. The first climb, out of the Buca Valley, is steady. Then it is down into the Sacapulas Valley, but the relief is only temporary: the next leg is a stiff 30-km (19-mile) ascent back into the Cuchumatanes Mountains. The terrain is formidable, and it is easy to understand why the Spaniards and more recently the Guatemalan government have struggled to control this region. Much of the area was razed during the civil war — evidence of which can still be seen — and then repopulated with 'model villages'. The colourful town of Nebaj is hidden at the bottom of a valley that is high in the mountains and often swathed in mist.

Day 11: Nebaj to Uspantán
40 km (25 miles); 7 hours cycling

This seriously remote, rugged and yet beautiful countryside was hard hit during the civil war. The route rolls up and down all day, crossing several river valleys, passing waterfalls and cloud forests, on dirt roads with only a tiny amount of traffic. The final downhill, to reach the tranquil town of Uspantán, is one of the longest and most satisfying of the trip.

Day 12: Uspantán to Cobán
64 km (40 miles); 8 hours cycling

Today you finally leave the mountains behind you. After crossing two passes you rejoin tarmac for the cruise into the imperial city of Cobán, surrounded by cloud forest and famed for its coffee and cardamom.

Day 13: Cobán to Lanquín
70 km (44 miles); 7 hours cycling

Remote dirt roads and jeep tracks lead through rolling hills to the sleepy town of Lanquín, the base for exploring Semuc Champey. This is a wonder of the world, a natural land bridge covered in gleaming water pools that spans the Cahabón gorge. Most people choose to spend the afternoon enjoying a leisurely picnic in this liquid paradise.

Day 14: Lanquín to Cobán

The morning is spent exploring the extraordinary limestone cave system around Lanquín before returning to Cobán.

Day 15: Cobán to Antigua

Transfer across central Guatemala to Antigua.

Day 16: Antigua

There is an optional ride up Volcan Fuego, but Antigua has many attractions to explore as well as being a shopper's paradise. In the evening it is time to celebrate the completion of this mighty trans-Guatemalan expedition.

Day 17: Departure

Transfer to Guatemala City for the flight back home.

CONTACT:
KE ADVENTURE TRAVEL
LAKE ROAD
KESWICK
CUMBRIA CA12 5DQ
UK
www.keadventure.com
tel: +44 (0)17687 73966

The Southern Highlands, Iceland

- Route rating: strenuous
- Off-road
- 9 days/8 nights
- Dates: July to August

Do you believe in fairies? Or elves? Or lovelings and dwarfs and goblins? If you do not, then read no further. If you do, then you really should bike across Iceland, for this is unmistakably the land of the 'little people'. The abundance of unfamiliar, jaw-dropping natural phenomena in this country — vast icecaps, geothermal pools, volcanic deserts, steaming volcanoes, congealed lava flows and fumaroles — is more redolent of a mythical kingdom, of Middle Earth perhaps, than of anywhere on this planet.

European perceptions of Iceland have been haunted by these awe-inspiring landscapes for centuries. Ancient Britons thought this was not only the brink of paradise (and that the Elysian Fields, Avalon or the Hesperides lay beyond), but also a land inhabited only by dog-headed people. To medieval Europeans it was the fire-belching gateway to hell. More recently, we have come to understand that Iceland is truly a paradise — for geologists, volcanologists and glaciologists. And looking at the landscape today, it is easy to see how it inspired centuries of myths.

One of the joys of this trip — an eight-day traverse of the southern highlands — is that the landscape changes continually. Highlights of Mother Nature's power include the waterfalls at Haifoss, active volcanoes, the clear and pure Arctic light, Eldgja Gorge, the Hrafntinnusker ice caves and the vast Vatnajokull icecap.

Iceland is very sparsely populated, and its road network amounts to a single band of tarmac around the coastal strip. This, then, is a real mountain-bike adventure for experienced cyclists. The surfaces you cycle on range from hard-packed jeep tracks to, well, no track at all: in some sections the footpaths or pony trails disappear altogether, and you have to follow your nose, bush-bashing on two wheels across the lunar landscape. But as well as mountains, ash deserts and many rivers to cross, you will also be treated to sections of single-track and fast valley descents. Daily distances are between 40 and 70 km (25–44 miles) — not overly long, but some days are tough. However, the near-constant daylight in July and August means there is always plenty of time to reach your destination. There is a support vehicle, but because of the terrain it is not always able to follow your route.

The weather in Iceland is notoriously unpredictable. That said, July and August are the most settled months, when it is reasonable to expect predominantly clear days with daily temperatures of 10–20°C (50–68°F). At night it drops to just above zero. Wild winds and rainstorms can cut through at any time, though, so it is important to come prepared for the full gamut of conditions, with a good set of waterproofs.

Accommodation outside Reykjavik is in mountain huts, a network of lodgings provided for walkers and bikers. The hut at Hrauneyjar is comfortable, with a bar and a restaurant. Elsewhere they provide basic dormitory accommodation, hot showers and cooking equipment. Meals are prepared by your support team.

Cosmopolitan delights are to be found only in Reykjavik, home to 62 percent of the population. Icelanders have something of a reputation for dourness and severity. As it happens, Reykjavik has a rather bohemian air, and on Saturday nights, when the local youth gambol from bar to club in a giddy display of weekly euphoria, you will scarcely see a frowning face. The trip starts and finishes with a Saturday night in Reykjavik, where alcohol and entertainment are not cheap; as you will not pass another shop in the entire week, however, you should have saved enough kronur to join in the mêlée.

GLACIERS, STEAMING VOLCANOES, GEOTHERMAL POOLS:

THE SCENERY IN ICELAND IS AWESOME

The Southern Highlands, Iceland

Day 1: Arrival in Reykjavik

Arrive at Keflavik airport and transfer (50 minutes) to the guesthouse in Reykjavik. The capital is easy and pleasant to walk around, and this is an opportunity to pick up any provisions you need for the week ahead. As this is Saturday night, it would be churlish not to experience a taste of the uninhibited nightlife.

Day 2: Reykjavik to Hrauneyar
40 km (25 miles); 3½ hours cycling

A three-hour transfer takes you over the Hellisheidi moorland and past Mount Hekla, an active volcano (you can warm your bottom on the top of it) that last erupted as recently as 2000, and was believed by 16th-century Europeans to be the entrance to hell, so often did it spout fire and ash. The journey brings you to the beginning of the ride at Holaskogur

hut. Immediately, the ride plunges off the tourist trail into the middle of nowhere, following a jeep track up to the spectacular waterfalls of Haifoss. The landscape changes from pasture to bleak scree, and you pick up a faint footpath down through the valley — this is fast, flowing single-track — to reach the old Viking settlement of Strong. Then it's all change again as you enter the beautiful Gjain Valley, a sort of giant version of the Yorkshire Dales, which leads back to tarmac and a roll down the road to the mountain hut at Hrauneyar.

Day 3: Hrauneyar to Holaskjol
70 km (44 miles); 7 hours cycling

This is a big day: a long ride with fantastic scenery. A decent jeep track leads into the Fjallabak Nature Reserve and on to the geothermal pools at

Landmannalaugar: the rhyolite peaks, lava flows and hot springs of this weird and colourful area are reason enough to stop you in your tracks, but there is also time before lunch for a bathe in the natural pools here. This is the steaming heart of the southern uplands and the afternoon ride undulates across compacted volcanic ash, over low passes, past fumaroles and in and out of 15 or more gorges cut with icy rivers. These rivers have to be crossed, which can take some bottle when they are thigh deep and nearly three metres (20 or so feet) across. A steep up and down brings you to Eldgja ('Fire Gorge'), a 40-km (25-mile) long volcanic rift. The final few kilometres follow the Skafta River, passing a series of cascades. You'll find the welcoming hut at Holaskjol a relief when it comes into sight at the end of this strenuous day.

Day 4: Blautulon and Eldgja Canyon loop
35 km (22 miles); 5½ hours cycling

You are almost guaranteed not to meet anyone on this horseshoe-shaped ride into the desolate wilderness to the north of the Holaskjol hut. The first goal of the day is the Noroariofaera Valley, from where a dirt track leads over to Lake Blautulon. A tough, but short, climb brings you out on a ridge at the head of Eldgja Canyon: here the magnificent views of Vatnajokull, the world's third largest icecap, are utterly heart-stopping. If all this is beginning to sound like a geography field trip, fear not: the afternoon is pure mountain biking, with two excellent descents.

Day 5: Holaskjol to Lake Alftavatn
55 km (34 miles); 7 hours cycling

Today's start should delight aficionados of single-track: a 15-km (9-mile) dash through the narrow Alftavatn gorge on an unused pony trail. This spills out on to another jeep track threading over the last of the Fjallabak hills, emerging dramatically onto a black desert of volcanic ash gashed by rivers and passing beneath the cliff faces of the Myrdalsjökull Icecap: yet more unearthly Icelandic scenery. Where water and ash meet, inevitably, the cycling gets tough, and there are five hard kilometres (three miles) before the surface gets firmer. A final climb brings you to the blue shores of Lake Alftavatn and the overnight hut.

Day 6: Loop ride (or trek) to Hrafntinnusker ice caves

This is effectively a rest day. However, few who have made it this far will need a rest, and there are a number of interesting options for exploring this swathe of Icelandic outback. A ride on a remote jeep track leads past hot springs and across more barren, lunar landscapes to the ice caves at Hrafntinnusker. Alternatively, you could walk part of what is undoubtedly destined to become one of the world's most renowned and popular long-distance treks, from Landmannalaugar to Skogar. Then there is the climb on to the snowfields of the Kalkadof Mountains, with a chance of reaching the summit of Mount Haskerdingur (1,281 m/4,203 ft). Of course, you could just spend the day lazing on the grass beside the lake.

Day 7: Lake Alftavatn to Thorsmork
35 km (22 miles); 7 hours cycling

The day's route follows the Landmannalaugar-to-Skogar trek at first, before peeling off at Hatfell. The scenery changes remarkably today, the boulder-strewn plateau giving way to alpine hills and (something you will not have seen much of all week) trees. This is a rolling day, heading south to emerge eventually, via dense birch forests and carpets of arctic flowers, in the Thorsmork Valley. Another geographical wonder, this spectacular valley surrounded by rivers and glacier-clad mountains is a favourite spot for weekenders from Reykjavik. Accommodation is in a hut at Thorsmork.

Day 8: Thorsmork to Reykjavik

The transfer back to Reykjavik takes two and a half hours, with a halt at the impressive Seljlandsfoss waterfall and the famous Blue Lagoon geothermal pools for a warming soak in the mineral-rich, milky waters. There is time to pack up the bikes at the guesthouse before heading out for another ripper of a Saturday night on the tiles of Reykjavik.

Day 9: Departure

The morning is free for shopping and sightseeing. Transfer to the airport in the afternoon.

CONTACT:
KE ADVENTURE TRAVEL
LAKE ROAD
KESWICK
CUMBRIA CA12 5DQ
UK
www.keadventure.com
tel: +44 (0)17687 73966

SELJLANDSFOSS WATERFALL

Leh to Manali, India

- Route rating: strenuous
- Mainly off-road (jeep tracks) with sections of tarmac
- 18 days/17 nights
- Dates: mid-July to mid-September

The bare statistics of this trip speak for themselves: 800 km (500 miles) in 11 days' cycling from Leh to Manali, across four massive Himalayan passes, with many strenuous ascents and swift descents through forbidding terrain. This is, beyond question, an epic journey.

The key to tackling a mountain ride of this magnitude is acclimatization, and to this end you spend the first third of the trip in the fascinating city of Leh (3,500 m/11,480 ft) adjusting to the altitude. Reminiscent of Kathmandu in the 1970s and full of cobbled streets, bazaars, the jangling of prayer wheels and the low hum of praying monks, Leh makes the perfect base for increasingly ambitious day rides to monasteries and palaces along the Indus Valley. The final day ride takes you to the top of the Khardung La, at 5,380 m (17,650 ft) the highest motorable pass in the world.

The great Leh to Manali highway crosses three distinct geographical zones: the barren Ladakh plateau, the semi-arid Lahaul Valley and the lush forested slopes of the Kulu Valley. A colossal feat of road engineering, it connects the Tibetan-influenced, Buddhist and brightly coloured mountain people with the Aryan Hindus of the plains.

The ride (daily distances are 40–80 km/ 25–50 miles) has a downhill trend, with some numbing descents, but there is plenty of work to do as well to get on top of the passes. A support vehicle (loaded with spare brake blocks) is ever-present and carries all the equipment needed for the nights camping in the wilds.

At the end of the ride there is time for a dose of luxury in Manali and Delhi. You may well need it.

THE ZANSKAR RIVER VALLEY – A FINE VIEW FROM THE SADDLE

Day 1: Arrival in Delhi
Arrive at Delhi airport, stay overnight.

Day 2: Fly to Leh
After the flight from Delhi to Leh, over the breathtaking massifs of Nun and Kun, you check into the small, family-run hotel. You can take the opportunity for a short afternoon walk around the main bazaar or through the Old Town. Only 50 years ago Leh was a key centre on two main trading routes, and its markets are still busy and colourful, thanks in part to the many Tibetan refugees who sell their craftwork and artefacts here.

Day 3: Ride to Stok Palace
13 km (8 miles); 3 hours cycling
Continuing the gentle acclimatization process, this is a short afternoon ride, mainly downhill, across the Indus River to Stok Palace, the vast residence of the former rulers of Ladakh. Here you can take a tour of the museum, with its fine views back towards Leh. The Indus, one of the world's great rivers, is young here yet still impressive, cutting a swathe through the arid plains and providing flashes of brilliant green in the predominantly brown landscapes.

Day 4: White-water rafting
Lazing in a raft is a fine way to acclimatize, and this four-hour trip, past villages and low-grade rapids to a gorge where the Indus and the Zanskar rivers meet, makes for an enjoyable morning. Anyone now itching to ride can choose to head off into the hills around Leh in the late afternoon.

Day 5: Ride to Hemis Monastery
25 km (16 miles); 3½ hours cycling
The morning ride follows the ancient road along the Indus Valley to the turning for Hemis. It is a stiff climb to the monastery, but the vehicle will scoop up anyone who does not feel ready for it. Built in the mid-17th century, this is the largest and richest of the central Ladakh Buddhist monasteries and the site of a famous summer festival. The ride back down to the river offers a small taste of the thrills that lie ahead on this trip. The vehicle takes you back to Leh.

Day 6: Ride on jeep road from Chilling
30 km (19 miles); 3 hours cycling
The ride starts at the remote village of Chilling (a two-hour vehicle transfer from Leh), start of the popular Markha Valley trek. The two-wheel descent, on a rough jeep track along the river, is a classic Himalayan ride through a rocky, barren landscape. From the main road you can ride the 37 km (23 miles) back to Leh, or hitch a lift in the vehicle.

Day 7: Khardung La Pass
90 km (56 miles); 7 hours cycling
This day is the finale to the acclimatization programme, and it's a humdinger: a climb up to and descent from the world's highest motorable pass. At 5,380 m (17,650 ft), the Khardung La is a mighty challenge. The road is not too steep, but the sun beats down relentlessly, and the altitude is testing. The views — south over the Zanskar range and north towards the towering Saser Spur and the peaks of the central Karakorams beyond — are sublime.

Day 8: Leh to Rumpsti
34 km (21 miles); 3 hours cycling

And so the great journey begins. To avoid retracing your steps, a vehicle transfer takes you to the checkpost at Upshi and the Manali turn-off. Two walls of rock flank the tarmac road that you cycle in the afternoon, which steadily climbs past small villages on the way to your destination, the little settlement at Rumpsti. The altitude here is high at 4,370 m (14,340 ft), and the views from the campsite are really quite magnificent.

Day 9: Rumpsti to Pang
95 km (59 miles); 8 hours cycling

The Taglang La — the second-highest motorable pass on the planet — beckons first thing this morning. The Leh to Manali highway is a truck route, so the 30-km (19-mile) climb is well graded, with a series of switchbacks leading to the flattish pass itself, which boasts a solitary *chai* (spice tea) shop. The views towards the snow-covered ranges on the southern side of the Himalayas are impressive and well worth a moment's rest. The terrain, meanwhile, remains windswept and bleak as you leave the pass to drop down to the Moray Plains, a continuation of the Tibetan plateau. After 35 km (22 miles), the road drops down again into a spectacular rift valley. The campsite lies near a road-workers' camp, on a riverbank beside the settlement of Pang (4,400 m/14,440 ft). Temperatures here can plummet as the sun drops and the brilliance of the mountain light slowly fades away.

MOUNTAIN VILLAGES ON THE LADAKH PLATEAU

Day 10: Pang to Sarchu
76 km (48 miles); 7 hours cycling

Another day, another Himalayan pass: two, in fact, as this hefty day in the saddle crosses both the Lachalung La (5,065 m/16,620 ft) and the Nakli La (4,900 m/16,080 ft). Above all else, though, this is a day for marvelling at the extraordinary adventure in engineering that created this road. In some places it seems to hang from the sky, while in others it cuts impossible paths through walls of rock, and throughout it is enlivened by bizarre Indian road signs. The climb up to Lachalung La is 30 km (19 miles) long but easy going all the way, and from the top you will be treated to a great view of the Nakli La. Though it looks a stone's throw away, it is in fact 6 km (3¾ miles) swiftly down and 8 km (5 miles) back up. Then the long descent kicks off properly, down an exhilarating switchback of 22 hairpin bends known as the Gata Loops (hardcore bikers can cut down more directly on road-workers' footpaths) to reach Brandy Nullah. The campsite for tonight's accommodation lies on the border between the states of Jammu and Kashmir and Himachal Pradesh.

Day 11: Sarchu to Jespa
75 km (47 miles); 7 hours cycling

The morning offers plenty of time to enjoy the ever-changing scenery during the two- to three-hour climb to Bara Lacha Pass (4,880 m/16,010 ft), where the fascinating regions of Spiti, Zanskar, Lahaul and Rupshu meet. You will also

PRAYER FLAGS ARE COMMON IN THE PREDOMINANTLY

BUDDHIST REGION OF LADAKH

RIDING ACROSS THE BARREN LADAKH PLATEAU

have time for a quick *chai* before embarking on another tremendous 45-km (28-mile) descent. Civilization starts to return, as you camp in the shaded gardens of the government resthouse beside the Bhaga River in Jespa, which offers the luxury of toilets.

Day 12: Jespa to Khoksar
55 km (34 miles); 6 hours cycling

You ride into a different world today, as the barren landscapes of the high mountain plateaus give way to green alpine peaks, fields, villages and Hindu temples. A surface of broken tarmac brings you to Keylong, the main town in Lahaul, and on to Tandi where you can stop for lunch. The approach to the checkpost at Khoksar, beneath the Rohtang Pass, feels like Switzerland.

Day 13: Khoksar to Manali
77 km (48 miles); 5 hours cycling

You may be relieved to hear this is to be the last climb of the trip; 20 km (12½ miles) to the final but not insignificant 3,990 m (13,090 ft) Rohtang Pass is followed by a whopping 52-km (32-mile) descent to the busy tourist town of Manali, and a soft bed in a comfortable tourist hotel awaits.

Day 14: Manali

A day to rest, or to explore the bazaars, temples and springs of Manali.

Day 15: Nalagarh Fort

An eight-hour drive brings you to Nalagarh Fort, a fascinating 15th-century palace beneath the Shivalik Hills that is now a hotel, for some well-earned rest and recreation.

Day 16: Train to Delhi

The Shatabadi Express from Chandigarh arrives in Delhi mid-afternoon. Accommodation is in the Imperial Hotel.

Day 17: Delhi

A day for sightseeing and shopping before the late transfer to the airport.

Day 18: Departure

Flights leave in the early hours of the morning.

CONTACT:
KE ADVENTURE TRAVEL
LAKE ROAD
KESWICK
CUMBRIA CA12 5DQ
UK
www.keadventure.com
tel: +44 (0)17687 73966

Yeats Country and South Donegal, Ireland

- Route rating: moderate
- On-road
- 9 days/10 nights
- Dates: May to September

Ireland has changed much in the past 20 years. A period of extraordinary economic growth and a revitalized sense of national identity have forged a new, modern Ireland for the 21ˢᵗ century. This is for the good. However, in the urgent pace of change some of the age-old charm of the Emerald Isle — that disarming ability to lighten the heart and relieve the stress of metropolitan toil — has been sacrificed.

Happily, it has been left largely intact in one area: the northwest corner. In Counties Donegal, Sligo, Leitrim and Fermanagh the charm of Ireland is still as ingrained and ingenuous as it ever was. The green and gold light on a hillside after a rainstorm, the long wait for a pint of Guinness to settle, the easy pace of the people, the tinder-dry wit, standing stones in the mist, a trout rising on a tobacco-coloured lough — life in this part of Ireland remains nourishing for the soul.

It is also a superb place for a bike ride. The lanes are quiet, the pubs are perhaps the most welcoming hostelries on the planet and the landscape is wonderful. The most striking aspect of the scenery is its variety: in one day you can ride through glaciated valleys, beside immense sandy strands, along sea cliffs and out onto deserted moorland. Not to mention the limestone caves, granite mountains, forests, rivers and innumerable loughs.

There is a special kind of intensity to the green of the Irish landscape, and there is a reason for this: it rains a lot. This is, after all, the Atlantic coast of the Celtic Fringe. As the old adage goes, 'When you can't see the mountains, it's already raining. When you can see the mountains, it's about to rain.' In my experience it is never actually that bad: you might hit a fortnight of sunshine or you might get all four seasons in one day, but it is best to pack a good-quality raincoat anyway.

This ride starts at Boyle and finishes in Carrick-on-Shannon; both towns have railway stations, so you can to and fro easily from Dublin. It is an unguided ride and you have maps and detailed directions to follow each day. Crucially, you do need the requisite level of mechanical competence to keep your bike rolling for nine days. People are remarkably helpful in rural Ireland, but much of the route is on single-lane tarmac roads that carry a tiny amount of traffic. In the main, you are reliant upon yourself.

It is a misconception to imagine that Ireland is a great expanse of flat bogland. It is a mountainous country, especially so in the northwest corner, and there are some challenging climbs, particularly in Donegal. But there are also some superb descents, invariably back to the ocean or down to a remote lough. And in a sense, this is Ireland all over for you: you have to take the uphill with the downhill, the discord with the *craic*, the rain with the sunshine, and potatoes with everything.

THE MIGHTY SEA CLIFFS AT SLIEVE LEAGUE, COUNTY DONEGAL

BENBULBEN, COUNTY SLIGO

Day 1: Boyle to Rosses Point
65 km (40 miles); 4 hours cycling

The ride begins in ruins, abbey ruins that is, in the town of Boyle near the Sligo/Roscommon border. The vestiges of the 12th-century Cistercian abbey, an interesting mixture of Gothic and Romanesque styles, are well kept and make a wonderful place to stretch your legs for the first time. Lough Key is the first lough of the day, with fine views from the road by the shore. After Lough Arrow the route heads north, through quiet countryside and the villages of Heapston and Riverstown to Lough Gill, immortalized by Yeats in 'The Lake Isle of Innisfree'. Dromahair, a sleepy market town, is a good place for lunch before climbing to skirt Sligo town. The last descent is to Rosses Point, the Atlantic and a glorious beach.

Day 2: Rosses Point to Ballyshannon
83 km (52 miles); 5–6 hours cycling

Yeats is inextricably linked with Sligo, and after an early morning dash through the deciduous woods around Glencar Lake, you come to his burial place in the churchyard at Drumcliff. The route then winds along the coast before approaching the great rock corries of Benbulben, Ireland's most memorable mountain. (There is an 11-km/7-mile extra loop around the Horseshoe Valley here – tough climbing repaid by spectacular views.) A sweeping descent brings you back to Mullaghmore (with refreshments at the Pierhead Hotel), where Lord Mountbatten was murdered in 1973. There is one last swerve inland to Lough Melvin, followed by a few miles of open countryside to reach Ballyshannon, a lively town with good restaurants and music.

Day 3: Ballyshannon to Ardara
69 km (43 miles); 5 hours cycling

The vast strand at Rossnowlagh is one of Ireland's finest surfing beaches, but you have to remind yourself that this is only the first stop of the day and it may be too early for a swim. It will almost certainly be too early for a pint, tempting though the Smugglers' Arms (famous for its Sunday music sessions) may look. Minor roads wind on past Murvagh Strand and into Donegal town, where there are plenty of places to stop and refuel. You will want to let your lunch settle — a tour of the castle and the craft market should suffice — before mounting your steed again for the first big climb: a 6.5-km (4-mile) haul into the remote Blue Stack Mountains. There are excellent views during the final act of the day — a descent back to the coast and the thriving town of Ardara. Accommodation is in Woodhill House, where the food is great and the welcome is as warming as a hot-water bottle.

Day 4: Loop through Glencolmcille and back to Ardara
86 km (54 miles); 5–6 hours cycling

They call County Donegal the 'Highlands of Ireland', and early on today you will know why. The climb up Glengesh Pass is seriously steep. Then it is down to Carrick and up again, to reach the mighty sea cliffs around Slieve League. The village of Glencolmcille (where St Colmcille, a monk of pre-eminent importance in the early history of Christianity in Britain, founded an abbey) offers a folk museum and a café and makes a welcome stop. This is also the heart of the Donegal 'Gaeltacht', where Irish Gaelic is still spoken. The route heads up again, across empty moorland, and down (in a flash) to the coast and the sea caves at Maghera strand. A few miles round the coast is Ardara, where there is a pub with your name on it.

SUNSET ON LOUGH MELVIN

Day 5: Ardara to Ballybofey
76 km (48 miles); 5 hours cycling

Glenties, where two glens converge, is the first town en route. A lovely, quiet coastal road then leads around the southern shore of Gweebarra Bay, through the Derryloughlin Forest to the village of Doocharry on the Gweebarra River. A spectacular valley – this is countryside to make your heart sing – strikes out for the mountains from here, passing between the rain-washed stacks of Slieve Snaght and the Glendowan range. The geography of this area is all about the fusion of water and mountains. They meet in the bog, of course, and you have to cross acres of blanket bog, alive with birdlife and dotted with piles of cut peat, before the long downhill to leave the Glenveagh National Park. You pick up the River Finn and head east to the twin towns (across the river) of Ballybofey and Stranorlar. Again, there is no shortage of entertainment, with music gigs every night of the week.

Day 6: Ballybofey to Belleek
62 km (39 miles); 3–4 hours cycling

The entire day is spent riding on very isolated backroads with no traffic. There are also no shops or pubs, so it is important to victual carefully before leaving in the morning. Once again, water is everywhere: Killeter Forest gives way to Lough Derg (a place of pilgrimage) and then to the Pullans, an expanse of bog with hundreds of tiny lakes. The destination today is the town of Belleek, famous for its pottery and home to the Carlton, a very friendly country hotel.

Day 7: Belleek to Belcoo
67 km (42 miles); 4 hours cycling

If you availed yourself of the renowned hospitality in the public houses of Belleek last night, you will have a rude awakening this morning: the first 5 km (3 miles) are up a steep hill to reach the Lough Navar Forest. There are fabulous views over Lough Erne and across Northern Ireland from the cliffs of Magho, before you turn south to Derrygonnelly for lunch. A gentle descent through Big Dog Forest, followed by a spectacular spin along the edge of Lough Macnean, account for the afternoon, as the route nips back and forth across the border between the Republic and Northern Ireland before finally coming to rest at the border itself in the village of Belcoo.

Day 8: Loop around the Cuilgach Mountains and back to Belcoo
86 km (54 miles); 5 hours cycling

A gradual climb to Bellavally Gap will iron out any tension in the muscles early on, and then it is a long coast down to the village of Swanlibar for lunch. You are near to the source of the mighty River Shannon here. A sharp up and down, over Slieve Rushen, brings you to the shores of Upper Lough Erne. Florence Court, a National Trust-owned stately home, and the Marble Arch Caves, limestone caverns that can be explored in a boat, might tempt you out of the saddle for an hour or two in the afternoon. There is a stretch of open country before the final descent back into Belcoo.

Day 9: Belcoo to Carrick-on-Shannon
78 km (49 miles); 4 hours cycling

After the town of Glenfarne you head out into very quiet countryside for the morning. A good spot for lunch is Drumkeeran, by the shores of Lough Allen. There is a long descent to Drumshanbo, and you cross the river a couple of times before arriving in the delightful and bustling town of Carrick-on-Shannon. Trains to Dublin run from here, but the music and the pubs should offer sufficient entertainment to detain you for one last night of the *craic*.

CONTACT:
IRON DONKEY BICYCLE TOURING
15 BALLYKNOCKAN ROAD
SAINTFIELD
CO. DOWN
N. IRELAND BT24 7HQ
www.irondonkey.com
tel: +44 (0)2890 813200

A STANDING STONE AT GLENCOLMCILLE

Tuscany by the Sea, Italy

- Route rating: easy
- On road
- 7 days/6 nights
- Dates: May to June, September to October

The Tuscan landscape is associated in most people's minds with hills, very steep hills, in fact: hills that professional cyclists might face with some trepidation. But fear not, for there is one corner of Tuscany that is as flat as unleavened bread. Abiding by the first principle of civilized cycle touring ('Don't climb a hill if you don't have to'), this ride heads initially for the coast and the fertile plain of the Maremma (actually a swamp until it was drained in the 19th century). The final few days explore the low hills around Magliano near the Umbrian border, but you should have acquired your cycling legs by then — and there is always a vehicle at hand to run you to the top.

Many fans of Tuscany argue that the quintessence of European civilization lies here. Historically, relationships between Tuscan artists and merchants and rivalries between its towns ensured that for centuries the duchy enjoyed a degree of influence that was disproportionate to its size and position. Nowadays the people of Tuscany have mastered the art of good living. The region's weather, fresh produce, fine wine and unhurried approach to life are all conducive to general wellbeing. And the point of this tour is to encourage just a little of this wellbeing to rub off on you.

The coast of southern Tuscany and its offshore islands have a strong association with the Etruscans, the mysterious civilization that dominated the area from 1000BC until Roman times, and the archaeological remains here date principally from this era. In their role as gateway to the eastern Mediterranean, fortified ports such as Talamone and Orbetello have attracted successive waves of invaders — Roman, Byzantine, Sienese, Spanish, Austrian and most recently English — and it is easy to see why.

Nonetheless, a tour through this area is more about natural beauty than about great historical monuments. The prevailing landscape of the Maremma (a nature reserve) is the now globally rare *maquis* (or *machair*) heathland, where myrtle blossom, purple juniper berries, hardy evergreen shrubs, holly oaks and sea pines abound. It also boasts strawberry trees (*Arbutus unedo*), midget palms and wild horses, which the local cowboys round up once a year for a rodeo.

As there is so much to see in a small area, the tour is based at only two hotels. The first of these is an agricultural estate in the Maremma, and the perfect place to learn about and experience the quality of the local food: you can explore the farm and try a cookery lesson one afternoon. Tuscan cuisine (based on the tradition of *cucina povera* or 'poor cooking') is unsophisticated, relying on the best ingredients simply prepared. *Acquacotta* (a vegetable broth), *cacciucco* (fish soup), *panzanella* (bread, tomato and onion salad), *bistecca* (T-bone steak) and *panforte* (a delicious almond, citrus and honey cake) are some of the regional specialities that you should not miss. Equally enjoyable is the local wine. The second hotel, accordingly, is situated on a wine estate near the village of Magliano. There will be times during this week when you can be forgiven for forgetting that you have to do any cycling at all.

TUSCANY IS RENOWNED FOR ITS WINES

Day 1: The Maremma Park
7 km (4 miles); ½ hour cycling

The group gathers at the station in Orbetello (90 minutes by train from Rome) and transfers (15 minutes) to Antica Fattoria La Parrina, the hotel for the next three nights. La Parrina is a working estate, producing wine, cheese, olive oil, vegetables, balsamic vinegar and flowers. Accommodation is in the main estate house. There is a short warm-up ride (a 7-km/4-mile loop that you can do as often as you like) through the surrounding countryside, which is flat and bordered by hills on three sides. Dinner — using produce from the farm and regional recipes — is at the hotel.

Day 2: Loop via the Maremma Park and Talamone
48 km (30 miles); 4 hours cycling

Today's route goes through the Albegna river valley away from your hotel and heads towards the coast. The route winds through the province of Grosetto, the agricultural heartland of this area, and there are wonderful views past vineyards, silvery olive groves and fields of watermelons. On the coast you come to the pretty fishing village of Talamone (supposedly named after one of the Argonauts who sailed with Jason in search of the Golden Fleece). There is a wealth of fascinating history here: the museum contains Roman archaeological remains (including a temple commemorating the momentous battle of Campo Reggio in 225BC between the Romans and the Celts); on the hill that looms above the village stands a 15th-century grey stone fortress; and in the main piazza stands a bronze bust of Garibaldi, who stopped here with his legion of Red Shirts on his way to liberate Italy. The clear-blue waters of the Tyrrhenian Sea might be too tempting to resist before you retire back to the hotel for some well-earned relaxation. Alternatively, you could time your return to fit in one of the afternoon cooking classes that the hotel has on offer to guests.

Day 3: Loop via Capalbio and Orbetello
55 km (34 miles); 5 hours cycling

You roll gently away from the hotel again this morning, across the Maremma and up to Capalbio. This hilltop town is encircled by a great wall along which you can wander, admiring the medieval centre, before descending to explore the cobbled streets and find a trattoria for lunch. You continue on towards the coast in the afternoon, passing through the hills above Ansedonia, where elegant modern villas are juxtaposed with excavations of the walls, gates and forum of a Roman town. There is a sand beach at the point where you reach the shining sea. Turning north, the route follows the coast through a heavily scented pine forest for 7 km (4 miles), following a cycling track — one of the most beautiful stretches of riding this week — to Orbetello. This town was badly bombed during the Second World War, but it has been reconstructed and today has a genial, sleepy air. It was built on a peninsula of sand and is connected by a bridge to the fist-shaped island of Argentario. Orbetello borders a lagoon that is home to a wealth of birdlife, including spoonbills, flamingos and many types of migratory ducks. There is time for a stroll around Orbetello and an ice cream (the best in Italy, some say) before transferring in the vehicle back to La Parrina.

TUSCANY IS FULL OF ELEGANT RELIGIOUS ARCHITECTURE

THE CLIFF-TOP TOWN OF PITIGLIANO

Day 4: Rest day

This day begins with a chance to get off-shore. The vehicle drops you in the village of Porto Santo Stefano (famous for its fish market), from where a ferry leaves for Giglio Island. Here a bracing hike from the port up to the fortified village of Giglio Castello is rewarded with fantastic views back to the mainland. The island is rugged and beautiful, and the fight to prevent development and retain its integrity is constant. Lunch on the beach is followed by a guided walk to discover more about the island's interesting and diverse flora. Back on the mainland you transfer into the hills to a new hotel: Fattoria di Magliano is a recently converted farmhouse, set among vineyards, on a hilltop near the village of Magliano. Dinner is at the hotel.

Day 5: Loop via Magliano and Pereta
45 km (28 miles); 4 hours cycling

This is perhaps the hardest day. The ride sets off across rolling hills, past fields of poppies and sunflowers and through the vineyards of Scansaso (famous for the red Morellino wine) to an olive mill. Over a picnic lunch members of the Andreini family will explain how extra virgin olive oil is produced. In the afternoon you pedal through the medieval walled town of Magliano. Anyone still full of running can pedal the few steep kilometres up to the neighbouring village of Pereta and back to the hotel. There is a session tasting the wines produced on the estate before dinner in an excellent restaurant in town, sampling regional specialities such as wild boar, porcini and ravioli stuffed with truffles.

Day 6: Loop via Pitigliano
32 km (20 miles); 4 hours cycling

Heading inland through the hills of the southern extremity of Tuscany, close to the Umbrian border, you reach a pick-up point where the road gets steep and gnarly. The vehicle brings you on the last leg to Pitigliano, a beautiful town cut into the tufa rock on top of a cliff, surrounded by spectacular gorges, terraced vineyards (a renowned white aperitif wine comes from here) and thickets of stunted trees. After lunch a local guide takes you on a tour of the medieval district, including the Palazzo Orsini, the synagogue and the sunken roads dug by the Etruscans. The vehicle then delivers you back to the hotel for a spruce-up before a final gastronomic feast at a restaurant in Magliano.

Day 7: Departure

The trip concludes with a two-hour transfer back to Rome.

CONTACT:

VBT

614 MONTON ROAD

BRISTOL, VT 05443-0711

USA

www.vbt.com

tel: +1 800 245 3868

The Celestial Mountains,
Kazakhstan / Kyrgyzstan

- Route rating: strenuous
- Mainly off-road (jeep roads and single-track)
- 15 days/14 nights
- Dates: June to September

The remote region of Central Asia, stretching from the Caspian Sea to Mongolia and from the forests of Siberia to the Hindu Kush, may with justice be viewed by the intrepid as a vast adventure playground of extraordinary potential. Opportunities for climbing, ski mountaineering and trekking are all exciting, but it is the possibilities it offers for off-road, long-range, wilderness mountain biking that really set the hearts of true adventurers racing.

The region is geographically diverse, with hostile deserts and huge expanses of treeless steppe, but this trip heads straight for the mountains. The Tien Shan (or 'Celestial Mountains') is a knot of numerous ranges that together form the lofty border between the former Soviet republics of Kyrgyzstan and Kazakhstan and the wasteland of Xinjiang province in western China: a rugged wilderness of glaciers, dashing rivers and peaks, rising in the Central Tien Shan to the mighty Pik Pobedy (7,439 m/24,410 ft) and Khan-Tegri (6,995 m/22,950 ft). This ride starts in the foothills, a short distance from Almaty, before rolling south towards the high peaks.

The riding, on hard-pack or gravel jeep tracks and little-used mountain paths, is tough. The trip is punctuated by two days at the mountain adventure base in the Karkara Valley, where you and your wheels will be lifted skywards in a helicopter, landing at the top of neighbouring peaks for some serious downhill thrills.

The trip starts and finishes in Almaty. This decidedly cosmopolitan city has a fundamentally Russian air, though it has modernized quickly. There is nothing you cannot buy here, and it is lively enough at night. By contrast, the countryside of both Kyrgyzstan and Kazakhstan is profoundly rural. Towns are scarce, villages are small and the way of life is simple and basic in a way that few Europeans would now recognize. Although the ride follows sections of what was once the Silk Route, any international influence this might once have brought to these Central Asian mountain redoubts has long since disappeared. The people are very friendly, however, and generally delighted to see you. I rode through this region on my own eight years ago, and I have seldom encountered a people who have so little and yet insist on giving so much.

The ride is fully supported for the entire Kazakhstan section by two large ex-Soviet army trucks: one to follow the riders and the other to head off to set up camp, often beside icy rivers in serene locations. Solar panels and portable showers notwithstanding, this is fairly basic camping, compensated for more than amply by the splendid isolation.

PEDALLING ALONG A JEEP TRACK INTO THE

TIEN SHAN MOUNTAINS

Day 1: Arrival in Almaty

You arrive in Almaty, the capital of Kazakhstan, and transfer to the hotel. The morning is free to wander through the tree-lined boulevards. After lunch a sightseeing tour takes you to the state museum and the Zenkov cathedral.

Day 2: Almaty to Batan

Transfer (three hours) to the village of Batan (1,800 m/5,906 ft). The campsite, where you set up bikes and prepare for the first ride, lies at the confluence of three rivers – the Turgen, Shen-Turgen and Kishi-Turgen. The scenery is rather like the lower Alps, with pine forests, green pastures and clear, fast-running rivers.

Day 3: Batan to Assy River
50 km (31 miles); 6 hours cycling

The ride starts off with a winding climb beside the Kishi-Turgen River. The jeep track passes through a narrow gorge that opens out to reach a broad plateau, at the top of which is the Assay Pass (2,650 m/8,694 ft). In this quintessentially rural, empty terrain, the only people you pass will be the odd family of Kazakhs on horseback. A fine, undulating and speedy descent leads to the Assy River and the village of the same name. The campsite is near the river, and with the hours left in the day the brave can swim in the bracing mountain waters. The trout fishing is good, too.

THE RUGGED WILDERNESS OF KYRGYZSTAN
IS A MOUNTAIN-BIKER'S DREAM

HELI-BIKING IN THE MOUNTAINS ABOVE KARKARA

Day 4: Assy River to Sary Bulak River
50 km (31 miles); 6½ hours cycling
The jeep tracks you follow on this trip vary from hard-pack (easy to ride) to gravel (more technically challenging). Today starts with a 7-km (4-mile) climb punctuated by sections of loose gravel that make reaching the Zambas Pass hard graft. You are rewarded by great views over the Zheniske Valley and the Kungei Alatau Mountains to the south. Here you are still in the foothills of the Celestial Mountains, and now the track you follow gets fainter, passing through fields of wild flowers, cresting a number of ridges and eventually bringing you to the Ashyk Dala plateau, from which there is a fast descent to the campsite on the Sary Bulak River.

Day 5: Sary Bulak River to Chilik River
40 km (25 miles); 5 hours cycling
The heat gets turned up today with the first major downhill blast of the trip. This is hard earned, however, by the 30-km (19-mile) climb that you will need to endure first, through the Kungei Alatau Mountains, a spur of the Tien Shan that stretches from Almaty to Lake Issyk-Kul. The last 7 km (4 miles) traverse a broad plateau with several false summits. Beware that the track then practically disappears in the thick grass before suddenly dropping down a precipitous ridge, the beginning of a long and enjoyable 11-km (7-mile) downhill cruise that finishes in the Chilik River valley.

Day 6: Chilik River to Zhaydak Bulak
60 km (37 miles); 5½ hours cycling
Only two generations ago, the people of Kazakhstan were entirely nomadic: even today they still build summer yurt camps. Their homesteads are basic, and ploughing is done with animals, and haymaking by hand. The route for today's cycling passes a few small villages on a broken and pot-holed tarmac road that can be tough riding. The road eventually leads over a series of small passes to Zhaydak Bulak. The campsite for tonight is near the Charyn canyon, a dramatic-looking piece of deep, steep-sided gorge cut into barren steppe that is also known as the 'Kazakh Colorado'.

Day 7: Zhaydak Bulak to Karkara mountain base
74 km (47 miles); 6 hours cycling

Today the trip heads deep into the highest and mightiest part of the Tien Shan Mountains. The morning ride takes you through the Karkara Valley, a broad green expanse of meadows carpeted with wild flowers and dotted with grazing herds at this time of year. This valley, which heads towards the point where China, Kyrgyzstan and Kazakhstan meet, once lay on the Silk Route. The road is relatively good, but there are plenty of opportunities to take single-track shortcuts if you wish, on footpaths that snake up and down the mountainside.

Days 8 & 9: Heli-biking from Karkara
40–50 km (25–31 miles); 5 hours cycling per day

You spend these two days at Karkara, the main base for mountaineering expeditions in the Central Tien Shan. Accommodation is in a number of permanent tents, and there is a restaurant and bar. Climbing teams are taken up by helicopter from here to the base camps on Khan Tegri and Peak Pobedy. On both days here, ex-Soviet troop-carrying helicopters will scoop you up to 3,500 m (11,480 ft) for a superb single-track descent back into the Karkara Valley. Weather and levels of fitness will determine which peak you land on, but the views are always sensational and the descents are sure to take your breath

away. On returning to camp you can have a sauna and a beer while reflecting on this question: heli-biking – how can you beat it?

Day 10: Karkara to Kokshar River
56 km (35 miles); 5 hours cycling

One of the great things about this trip is that the cycling just keeps on getting better and better as the days go by. The road this morning follows the Karkara Gorge to the confluence with the Kokshar River. There are several rivers to wade through, and then the track dwindles steadily until you are simply biking across wilderness. The river is your guide, and you eventually emerge at a campsite beneath a memorial to an early explorer of the Celestial Mountains.

OPPOSITE: NOMADISM IS STILL A WAY OF LIFE
FOR MANY KYRGYZ

RIGHT: A KYRGYZ SHEPHERD

Day 11: Kokshar River to Saary Zhaz River 48 km (30 miles); 5½ hours cycling

This is probably the best day of the trip for biking, and the mountain scenery is awesome. A short punch uphill is followed by a long climb through a valley to reach the Mingtur Pass (3,900 m/ 12,800 ft), where a range of 6,000 m (19,700 ft) snow-capped peaks, including the spectacular black pyramid of Khan-Tengri, suddenly comes into view. A long cross-country descent follows. You rejoin a road at the Saary Zhaz River and follow it for 20 km (12½ miles) of undulating single-track to the remote and rarely used (certainly by Westerners) border crossing at Echkilitash. The campsite is a short distance into Kyrgyzstan, in a glorious riverside position.

Day 12: Saary Zhaz River to Lake Issyk-Kul 70 km (44 miles); 6 hours cycling

In the morning the road rises and falls beside the river with a general trend downhill: this is a lovely ride that rolls into a tight canyon. At the junction with the Ottyk River the 30-km (19-mile) climb (mainly on tarmac) starts, winding slowly away into the far distance and gently uphill to reach the Chon Ashy Pass, nearly 1,200 m (4,000 ft) above. After lunch one of the best downhills of the entire trip brings you crashing down into the upper valley of Issyk-Kul. The camp tonight is beside the Saary Zhaz River just past the Kyrgyzstan border post of Echkilitash.

Day 13: Return to Almaty

The long bus journey back to Almaty takes most of the day, with a lunch stop at Karkara. When you finally arrive, there is time for a shower before heading out to experience a little Kazak nightlife.

Day 14: Almaty

This is a free day, but a trip to the central market should not be missed. Transfer to the airport in the early hours of the morning.

CONTACT:
KE ADVENTURE TRAVEL
LAKE ROAD
KESWICK
CUMBRIA CA12 5DQ
UK
www.keadventure.com
tel: +44 (0)17687 73966

High Atlas Traverse, Morocco

- Route rating: strenuous
- Off-road
- 10 days/9 nights
- Dates: May, June and September

Twenty years ago, Morocco was the first exotic mountain-biking destination. It remains a superb place to bike today, and this tour I heartily recommend, as it captures much of the adventure that the early riders on their heavy, boneshaking, suspension-less machines originally went in search of. The network of tracks (or *pistes*) — either old Berber trade routes or imperial roads created during attempts to pacify the southern tribes — that criss-cross the Atlas Mountains are perfect for mountain biking, enabling you to visit remote parts of the lofty interior that no one else can reach.

The trip starts and finishes in Marrakech, the former capital of the Berber people and the most sensuous and exciting city in North Africa. The majority of the riding, however, is far away from urban life, high up in the mountainous heart of the country, among the mud kasbahs and the soaring peaks in the wilds of the Central High Atlas and the Middle Atlas ranges.

These peaks may look forbidding and inhospitable, but the people are by contrast warm and welcoming. A journey like this through central Morocco is as much about experiencing the culture as it is about the wilderness. The indigenous Berber people of the High Atlas relinquished their feudal way of life only in the mid-20th century, and they have held on to many traditional practices. They are an open, friendly people, and the women usually go about unveiled. This trip finds a good balance between hotels, camping in remote locations and staying in small but basic village gîtes or kasbahs (the fortified, mud-built houses that are such a distinctive architectural feature of the Atlas). You can be sure that authentic traditional hospitality will envelop you at some stage on this ride.

It is tough biking terrain: the tracks are mostly vehicle width and rough in places. There are lots of long, hard ascents (4 km/ 2½ miles in total over the trip) but most of them are optional. A Land Rover will be on your tail for almost the entire journey, and an experienced mountain-biking guide will lead the way. Some of the downhills are legendary. The daily distances increase as the tour goes on, with an average of 65 km (40 miles) and a total of 450 km (280 miles) for the whole trip. The high temperatures (the days are mainly clear and nights can be cold) add to the pain, and you do need to be fit to enjoy this trip, just as you need a good set of wheels. But it is all worth it: no one who rides the off-road descent along the old Berber trail from Ameniter to Aït Ben-Haddou will ever forget it; the hues of the desert kasbah at Telouet are mesmerizing; the contrast of virid terraces and bare rocks in Dadès Gorge is the stuff of a child's imagination; the sheer natural splendour of the Bou Gamez Valley will make you reel; and, sitting around a campfire eating a traditional Moroccan dinner and admiring the starry heavens, you will be already planning your return.

THE RUINS OF A KASBAH IN THE DADES GORGE

Day 1: Arrival in Marrakech

Arrive in Marrakech. Transfer to the hotel near the Djemaa El Fna, one of the most charismatic market squares on the planet. At night it teems with an extraordinary array of acts, characters and street vendors, including snake charmers, storytellers, scribes, tooth-pullers, musicians, pickpockets (of course), trance-healers, clowns, child boxers and acrobats. The Djemaa El Fna is endlessly fascinating, and you will want to return to it again and again.

Day 2: Marrakech to Tijhza
25 km (15½ miles); 3 hours cycling

After a leisurely breakfast and a session putting the bikes together, there is a 3-hour vehicle transfer along good roads southeast to the summit of the Tizi n'Tichka. This 2,260 m (7,417 ft) pass, built by the French when pacifying the unruly tribes of southern Morocco, leads into the heart of the High Atlas and is an excellent place to begin the ride. The rough tarmac road heads spectacularly down to Telouet, where there is time to admire the Glaoui Kasbah, one of the most amazing edifices in the Atlas. On the final leg to Tijhza the road turns into a dirt track (or *piste)*, a good introduction to the terrain. Accommodation is in a traditional Moroccan house converted into a mountain gîte, where it is possible to sleep on the roof to savour the stars.

ON THE TRAIL IN THE HIGH ATLAS

Day 3: Tijhza to Boumalne de Dadès
45 km (28 miles); 5 hours cycling

The mountain biking begins for real today. An undulating mule track snakes away from Tijhza, along a river valley and through scattered Berber communities. There are fast sections, a few bracing river crossings and one gnarly descent. The landscape is spectacular — green terraces, steep gorges and wonderfully coloured scree slopes — all the way to Aït Ben-Haddou, where the tarmac resumes. This is the site of a stunning kasbah, piled up on a dark shaft of rock, that has been used in numerous films, including *Gladiator* and *Lawrence of Arabia*. After lunch a 2½-hour transfer heads through the Dadès Valley, where smaller kasbahs abound. The terrain changes as you skirt Jebel Sahro, an immense and barren semi-desert that stretches away south to the Sahara. A swim at the hotel will be welcome before you sit down for a dinner of tagine and kebabs.

Day 4: Boumalne de Dadès to Tizi n'Ouano
40 km (25 miles); 5½ hours cycling

The route turns north, heading back into the High Atlas through the Dadès Gorge, a lush, finely carved limestone valley. After a 45-minute transfer, at the point where the tarmac runs out and the valley narrows, it is time to get back in the saddle for the ride into the mountains above Msemir. A fast, rolling, mainly uphill track leads to the base of Tizi n'Ouano, where the major challenge of the day begins — a tough 15-km (9-mile) climb to the pass. The Land Rover behind will collect those who flag. From the top,

there is a brief descent to the remote campsite. There is usually a shepherd about who will sell your cook a sheep to spit-roast on the fire.

Day 5: Tizi n'Ouano to Lake Isli
50 km (31 miles); 7 hours cycling

Today's ride follows a hard, exciting route with a number of big downhills: a highlight of the trip for keen mountain bikers. After breakfast a massive descent leads to the friendly mountain village of Agoudal, where the road surface improves. This is the beginning of a fertile plain across which the road, with tarmac sections, follows river courses flanked by fields. At Imilchil, a village still steeped in Berber customs and the site of the famous September marriage festival, there is another ornate kasbah. Whooping children will most likely welcome you and see you off on the final leg of the day, eastwards to a campsite beside Lake Isli.

Day 6: Lake Isli to Anergui
50 km (31 miles); 7 hours cycling

Another full-on day of adventure in the Moroccan wilderness involving river crossings, single-track trails and sections where there is no trail at all. A high-speed downhill plunges into an area of national forest that leads to a gorge with a waterfall, followed by a technical (difficult) climb before lunch in a green valley. In the late afternoon a slow, even climb leads to a thunderous 1 km (½-mile) descent to the isolated mountain gîte, where there is a hammam or steam bath in which to relax. Dinner this evening is a traditional village feast.

CONES OF SPICES IN THE MARKET, MARRAKECH

Day 7: Anergui to Zaouia Ahansal
60 km (37½ miles); 7 hours cycling

All morning you follow a river through a gorge that snakes into the heart of the Middle Atlas range on an undulating, rough track. Lunch (and a snooze) precede an optional 10-km (6-mile) climb that begins at the towering limestone sculpture called Cathedral Rock and rises into a forest of cedar and juniper. The forests provide an atmospheric contrast to the aridity of the mountains, rich in birdlife, wild flowers and butterflies, as well as home to Barbary apes. Not that you should be concentrating on anything but the trail during the crashing 15-km (9-mile) descent on forest track — one of the best descents of the trip. The gîte for the night is in a magical spot beside the old kasbah in Zaouia Ahansal.

Day 8: Zaouia Ahansal to Marrakech
40 km (25 miles); 5 hours cycling

The last day of cycling kicks off with a 27-km (16³/₄-mile) climb, gaining 1300 m (4,270 ft). It is optional (phew!), and those who decline the pain can relax or explore Zaouia Ahansal. You regroup at the top of the pass, from which there are views over a barren land, inhabited only by nomadic herders, towards the sacred peak of Jebel Mgoun (4,079 m/13,382 ft), Morocco's second-highest peak outside the Toubkal massif. The descent into the Bou Gamez valley is a white-knuckle affair. On the valley floor tarmac is back, making for a high-speed cruise the length of the valley to meet the vehicles for the transfer back to Marrakech. After a clean-up and a brush-down, dinner is at a rooftop restaurant overlooking the Djemaa El Fna.

Day 9: Marrakech

There is an optional guided tour of the souks in the morning. Otherwise the day is yours, free to explore the city, haggle for a carpet, go for a ride or simply relax and lounge by the pool.

Day 10: Departure

Transfer to the airport for your flight.

CONTACT:
EXODUS TRAVELS
GRANGE MILLS
WEIR ROAD
LONDON SW12 0NE
UK
www.exodus.co.uk
tel: +44 (0)870 240 5550

OPPOSITE: THE DJEMAA EL FNA IN MARRAKECH
TEEMS WITH ACTIVITY AT NIGHT

Lhasa to Kathmandu, Nepal / Tibet

- Route rating: strenuous
- Off-road (95% on dirt roads)
- 21 days/20 nights
- Dates: end of July to September

The merest whisper of the name 'Tibet' is enough to set the pulses of travel aficionados racing. For years it was considered forbidden fruit to all but the most adventurous. Today there are fewer travel restrictions, but Tibet remains geographically inaccessible, cold, aloof and forbidding. The Tibetan people are largely semi-nomadic pastoralists, and their stoic character reflects the inhospitable nature of the landscape, effectively one vast, barren plateau at an altitude of over 4,000 m (13,100 ft). The 'roof of the world' is a hostile environment where life is short on luxury but correspondingly long on adventure. As they say, you don't go to Tibet: it calls you.

Nepal, by contrast, is lush, increasingly cosmopolitan and comfortable. There has been concern recently over travelling here but as part of a group it remains safe and easy, and you will meet hordes of fellow travellers. Successful architectural restoration programmes and a growing number of mountain environmental projects suggest that the Nepalese are becoming quite canny when it comes to tourism.

The two countries are connected by the 'Friendship Highway', a 920-km (570-mile) mainly dirt road that weaves southwest of Lhasa over a series of high-altitude passes to confront the north face of Everest and the full might of the central Himalayan range, before dropping off the plateau like a cascading stream to plunge 4,000 vertical metres (13,100 ft) to the Kathmandu Valley. By any standards, riding the Friendship Highway is an epic journey: a huge, high-altitude challenge.

On the way you may have to deal with fatigue, altitude sickness, poor diet, stomach bugs, sunstroke, a battered bike, dodgy toilets and even bandits. But the sense of achievement and the rewards gained are correspondingly great: you visit a handful of the most remarkable Buddhist monasteries on the planet, the scenery is simply astonishing, you ride down to the famous Everest Base Camp, and on one breathtaking day you descend continually for 160 km (100 miles). Can you beat that? This ride may not appeal to all, but for those who seek adventure, there is no other.

THE TOWERING HEART OF THE HIMALAYAS, SEEN FROM NEPAL

Day 1: Arrival in Kathmandu

Arrive in Kathmandu and transfer to the hotel. There is time to explore a little of this surprisingly urbane city before an evening briefing about the trip ahead.

Day 2: Kathmandu to Nagarkot
38 km (24 miles); 3 hours cycling

After an early breakfast the first ride heads east along the fertile Kathmandu Valley — the heartland of Nepal — to Bhaktapur, an ancient city and former capital of the valley. An earthquake here in 1934 ruined much of the medieval centre but a careful restoration project has followed: today magnificent temples and brick lanes lined with street vendors offer a fine insight into Newari culture. The quiet road to Nagarkot climbs steadily through terraced farmland for 20 km (12 miles) to reach the top of the valley, where there are impressive views of the Himalayan range. Accommodation is in a guesthouse on the valley rim.

Day 3: Nagarkot to Kathmandu
34 km (21 miles); 2½ hours cycling

The day kicks off with a serious descent on jeep tracks as far as the village of Shanku and then on to the Boudhanath Stupa. The intermittent cacophony of horns, drums and the fragrance of incense hint at the significance of this huge white-washed dome, the spiritual centre for Tibetan refugees and a draw for Buddhists from all over the world. The final few kilometres of riding bring you back to the hotel in the Thamel district of Kathmandu.

Day 4: Kathmandu to Lhasa

The early morning flight over the Himalayas to Gonggar airport has to rank as one of the most dramatic short flights on the planet. It is followed by a 90-km (56-mile) transfer to the small hotel in the colourful Tibetan quarter of Lhasa and a short ride round the capital.

Days 5, 6 & 7: Lhasa

In a sense, having to take three days to acclimatize to the altitude of the Tibetan plateau (Lhasa lies at 3,680 m/12,070 ft) is an opportunity: it would be far too easy to miss the extraordinary delights of this once forbidden city, the soul of Tibet, in the anxiety to get the wheels turning on the road. You really should visit the Potala Palace, a huge ochre fortress that dominates the city skyline. It is one of the architectural wonders of the world, and, whatever one might think of the Han Chinese presence in Tibet, a visit is imperative. The golden-roofed Jokhang Temple — a shrine for 1,300 years and home to a wealth of Tibetan treasures — and the Norbulinka Palace should not be missed either.

Day 8: Through the Lhasa Valley
45 km (28 miles); 3 hours cycling

Finally it is time to roll out of Lhasa and onto the Friendship Highway. The first stop, 7 km (4 miles) west of the city, is Drepung Monastery, home to a huge and influential monastic population before the Cultural Revolution. It remains an important pilgrim site. In the afternoon the route follows the broad expanse of the Lhasa River to a small guesthouse on its banks.

THE POTALA PALACE IN LHASA

DESCENDING FROM PANG LA, ACROSS THE HIGH DESERT OF SOUTHERN TIBET

Day 9: Lhasa Valley to Nagatze
55 km (34 miles); 5 hours cycling

Today you cross the first of the major passes on the Tibetan plateau, a mighty feat of endurance for all but the fittest. A Land Cruiser is on hand to gather up mere mortals. From the summit of Kamba La (4,794 m/15,730 ft), where prayer flags snap in the wind, the views of Nojin Kangstang (7,191 m/23,590 ft) in the distance and the turquoise jewel of Yamdok Lake at your feet are stunning. Then you hammer 300 vertical metres (980 ft) down to the lakeside and cruise round to the village of Nagatze.

Day 10: Nagatze to Gyantse
60 km (37 miles); 6 hours cycling

It is all uphill to the Karo La (5,045 m/ 16,550 ft), where you must test your brakes as the downhill is a screamer: 1,000 vertical metres (3,280 ft) into the Nyang Chu Valley and the town of Gyantse. Among the wonders to visit here is the massive tiered Kumbum Chörten, where Colonel Francis Younghusband established a garrison during the controversial British invasion of Tibet in 1904, a 'terrible and ghastly business' according to his own account. The town remains staunchly Tibetan.

Day 11: Gyantse to Shigatse
50 km (31 miles); 4½ hours cycling

The Tibetan plateau is one of the most ferocious environments in which to live, and indeed to cycle across, but there is some respite first thing today in the form of an 80-km (50-mile) transfer to the ornate 11th-century Shalu Monastery. After a picnic lunch you continue to ride on to Shigatse, Tibet's second-largest city, which has been a very important trading centre for centuries. You should try to shake off any fatigue to visit the Tashilhunpo Monastery, home of the Pachen Lama.

Day 12: Shigatse to Lhatze
65 km (41 miles); 6 hours cycling
Another day, another Tibetan pass: Tsuo La is reached by a long, gradual climb. Descent (on a reasonable dirt road) is excellent.

Day 13: Lhatze over the Gyatso La
60 km (37 miles); 5 hours cycling
You may sense that the mountains are drawing nearer, but they remain out of sight on the long climb to Gyatso La, at 5,220 m (17,130 ft) the highest pass on the Friendship Highway. This is a tough climb, followed by a rough ride down, and strictly for hard-core cyclists.

Day 14: Into the Rongbuk Valley
70 km (44 miles); 7 hours cycling
Reaching the top of Pang La (5,200 m/17,060 ft) you have to stop, not to catch a few breaths but rather to digest the full majesty of the Himalayan panorama, for here the roof of the world is spread before you. Eat your lunch and marvel. The afternoon is again spent tearing downhill, this time on a rough track into the famous Rongbuk Valley.

Day 15: Rongbuk Valley to Everest Base Camp
40 km (25 miles); 5 hours cycling
Cycling beneath the north face of Everest is one of the highlights of this remarkable two-wheel adventure. The road leads down past the Rongbuk Monastery and across glacial moraine to the Everest Base Camp, first used by Mallory and Irvine on the ill-fated 1924 expedition. There are a couple of permanent structures and usually a collection of expedition tents, but it is the atmosphere of the place that will hit you. Accommodation is back at the monastery.

Day 16: Rongbuk Monastery to Tingri
65 km (40 miles); 6 hours cycling
Heading back out of the broad Rongbuk Valley, you pick up the Friendship Highway again, cross the Nam La and head down to Tingri, the last major stop-off point for travellers heading south out of Tibet. The ruined fortress here is a reminder of the 18th-century Nepalese invasion. The views from the settlement, across a barren plain to Cho Oyu, are superb.

Day 17: Tingri to Nayalam
45 km (28 miles); 5 hours cycling
There are two high passes to cross today, so a transfer to the top of the first, Lalung La (4,850 m/15,910 ft), seems reasonable, before whooshing down and toiling back up to the last pass Tibet has to offer. At 5,050 m (16,570 ft), this is some spot for a picnic, with breathtaking views over the Shishipangma massif. The gap in the mighty Himalayan dentures is your exit route from the plateau. Set your altimeters here — it is 4,000 vertical metres (13,120 ft) down into Nepal — and keep your eyes peeled, as now you are in Yeti country.

Day 18: Nayalam to Dhulikhel
160 km (100 miles); 4 hours cycling
This is the day you have been waiting for, with 160 km (100 miles) of unbroken downhill. Yes, 160 km! Down, down you go through the Chinese customs post at Zhangmu (positioned precariously on the edge of a steep ridge), round endless hairpin bends in no-man's land, over the Kodari Bridge into Nepal and on, through a scented green world to Dolalghat. A transfer takes you to your guesthouse in lively Dhulikhel.

Day 19: Dhulikhel to Kathmandu
25 km (16 miles); 2 hours cycling
Dhulikhel is famed for its views of the spectacular sunrises over the mountains: if you are up early enough, the best place to catch one is the Kali Shrine, a 45-minute hike from town. An easy ride through the greenery of the valley brings you back to Kathmandu and a feast to mark the completion of this epic ride.

Day 20: Departure
Transfer to the airport for the flight home.

CONTACT:
EXODUS TRAVELS
GRANGE MILLS
WEIR ROAD
LONDON SW12 0NE
UK
www.exodus.co.uk
tel: +44 (0)870 240 5550

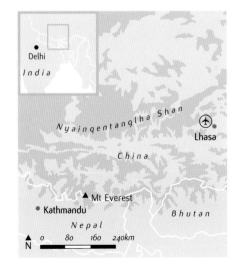

TERRACED LAND IN THE KATHMANDU VALLEY

Nelson to Queenstown,
New Zealand

- Route rating: moderate
- On-road
- 13 days/12 nights
- Dates: January to February

If the gods rode bikes (and who's to say they don't?), they would probably pedal down the west coast of New Zealand's South Island. There is nowhere else like it on the planet. Comparisons struggle to describe this region, but imagine a bit of Scotland and a bit of Washington State, juxtaposed with the French Alps and some Sumatran rainforest, all crammed into a slim strip of land facing the might of the Southern Ocean. Such is the glory of this scenery that, when you are riding along the West Coast, you can be forgiven for the fleeting feeling that you might just be a little god-like yourself.

The ride starts in the laid-back town of Nelson. From Westport to Haast it rolls alongside or near the ocean before turning inland to cross the mountain divide and then winds through the lakes to reach the buzzy adventure capital of Queenstown. With more than 750 km (470 miles) to pedal in ten days, this ride is no breeze. However, the group organizers offer different distance options for each day, and the support vehicle is never far away, so be assured that you can tailor the ride to your ability. Part of me says you should ride every metre, so scenic is the route. Yet there is so much of interest to stop and see along the way, and so much to do on the rest days, that you want to be feeling chipper enough to appreciate it all, and not flattened by overexertion.

You do not get breathtakingly dramatic coastal scenery like this without one essential ingredient, of course — heavy weather. The West Coast of the South Island is situated in the very southerly latitudes (there is nothing but empty ocean between here and Patagonia), and the weather is dominated by the 'roaring forties', the stormy west winds that tear up from the South Atlantic. All of which means it rains here (a lot), so be prepared; take waterproofs and the will to do battle with the weather should it cut up rough. But you can be lucky and miss it. I did. In the two weeks I took to ride from Nelson to Queenstown, the skies didn't spill a drop. The hot sun shone down every day on me, my bike, the improbably beautiful scenery and the highway of the gods.

THE INCREDIBLE LANDSCAPES OF THE SOUTH ISLAND'S WEST COAST

THE ROAD WINDS TOWARDS MOUNT COOK

Day 1: Arrival at St Arnaud

Meet in the sunny town of Nelson for a one-hour transfer to your hotel at St Arnaud, in the Nelson Lakes National Park. After the bikes have been fixed up, there is time for a walk down to Lake Rotoiti or through one of the glorious beech forests that prevail in the park. Or you may want to soak the journey away in a hot tub. There is a trip-orientation talk in the evening before dinner.

Day 2: St Arnaud to Gowan Bridge on the Buller River

32 km (20 miles); 2 hours cycling

Lake Rotoiti is the source of the Buller, New Zealand's fastest free-flowing river. The ride this morning follows it through forests of mountain, black and silver beech as far as Gowan Bridge. Here you exchange Lycra for a wetsuit and jump aboard a raft for a trip down the river. This stretch is Class III, fine for novices and very beautiful. A one-hour transfer brings you back to St Arnaud.

Day 3: St Arnaud to Westport

88 km (55 miles); 6 hours cycling

A 30-minute transfer drops you in Murchison, a former gold-mining town and now something of an adventure centre, where you start the ride. And some ride it is: the Buller River has carved out a deep gorge that is especially dark and forbidding on a grey day. You wheel past craggy precipices, primeval ferns and cabbage trees. At Hawks Crag the road has been literally blasted out of the rock. To call the Buller Gorge atmospheric is an understatement. This is a rolling ride and there are a couple of testing climbs before you spill out beside the ocean at Westport, the first European settlement on the West Coast and still a working coal town. If you have the time and the legs, Tauranga Bay has a seal colony and a beautiful beach.

Day 4: Westport to Greymouth
99 km (62 miles); 7 hours cycling
The fabled ride along the west coast of the South Island begins for real today. At times the views will leave you slack-jawed. The road is periodically reminiscent of the dreamy Californian Highway through Big Sur, and the untamed beaches you ride past – Tiromoana, Ten-Mile, Barrytown, Nine-Mile and Rapahoe – are an awesome reminder that the winters here are wild. The first stop is Charleston, a heaving shanty town during the gold rush 130 years ago, and now a quiet backwater. The vegetation turns semi-tropical as you approach Punakaiki and Pancake Rocks, with strange stacks of limestone on the shore that spurt geysers of seawater at high tide. The Paparoa Mountains loom to your left as you approach Greymouth, the largest town on the West Coast.

Day 5: Greymouth to Harihari
110 km (69 miles); 7½ hours cycling
There is some respite this morning: a flat road leads from Greymouth past miles of salt spray and lines of driftwood to the delightfully named town of Hokitika, a major centre for the working of jade. In

PANCAKE ROCKS AT PUNAKAIKI

the afternoon the ride returns to the hills, first across sheep-farming country and then through dense rainforest. Approaching the small town of Harihari, you can make out the faint shapes of the snow-capped Alps far away to the south.

Day 6: Harihari to Franz Josef Glacier
62 km (39 miles); 3½ hours cycling
The ride today brings you into the very heart of the West Coast. The scenery is amazing. A gradual climb over Mount Hercules is followed by a fast, twisting downhill to reach a river-streaked plain that leads into Westland National Park. Here vast rivers of blue ice, flanked by temperate rainforest, edge down almost to the ocean. Geographical diversity is matched by fascinating flora, as you ride past native forests of rata, kahikatea and flaming red rimu. The birdlife is rich, too: native parakeets, tui, tomtits, white herons and kiwis are all to be found here. The main draw, though, is the glaciers. Nowhere else in the world, at this latitude, do glaciers creep so close to the sea. Accommodation is in the Franz Josef Glacier Hotel, with views over the mighty ice river itself.

SHEEP BEING HERDED, SOUTH ISLAND

Day 7: Rest day in Franz Josef

If you want to get to know your bergschrunds from your seracs, this is a day for you. There are various ways to get up close to the Franz Josef Glacier — scenic flights, heli-hiking or a guided walk on the terminal face — all of which are fascinating experiences and can be easily arranged. The surrounding area also offers plenty of other more leisurely walks, as well as riding, fishing and bird-watching trips. With so many activities on offer, it should be a busy enough rest day.

Day 8: Franz Josef to Lake Moeraki
113 km (71 miles); 8 hours cycling

The ride south to Fox Glacier takes in a couple of big climbs. An optional detour to Lake Matheson offers the opportunity to admire with your own eyes one of the iconic images of New Zealand: the mountain peaks reflected in the lake. The Southern Alps are fixed in your sights for much of the rest of the day, on the long, flat pedal to Lake Moeraki, a tranquil loch surrounded by forest.

Day 9: Rest day in Lake Moeraki

You are now on the edge of the Haast area, a remarkable wildlife refuge comprising vast wetlands juxtaposed with rainforest, now protected as a World Heritage Site. Again, the choices for a day out of the saddle are plentiful, including canoeing, trout fishing, a guided walk to see the penguin colony and fur seals on Munroe Beach, and snorkelling (to name only a few).

The map shows:

New Zealand

Christchurch

• Nelson

Tasmin Sea

• Westport

Westland Bight

• Greymouth

• Franz Josef Glacier

• Christchurch

Haast

Lake Wanaka

Canterbury Bight

• Queenstown

• Dunedin

South Pacific Ocean

• Invercargill

0   80   160   240km

N

THE COAST ROAD NEAR HAAST

Day 10: Lake Moeraki to Lake Wanaka
180 km (112 miles); 9 hours cycling

This is a huge day with plenty of climbing — not that you have to ride all of it, of course. The road heads back to the coast and the rocky bluffs at Knight's Point before veering inland along the Haast River. The steep climb up to Haast Pass (563 m/1,847 ft) is what Kiwis call 'hard yakka'. The vegetation changes dramatically as you cross the mountain divide and enter Mount Aspiring National Park: this is sparse hill country, studded with raging waterfalls. It is still jaw-droppingly beautiful. The road glides around the edge of the powder-blue lakes, Hawea and Wanaka. A hot tub and a glass of local wine at the Edgewater Resort will be a welcome treat at the end of this massive day.

Day 11: Rest day at Lake Wanaka

It almost goes without saying that a huge variety of adventurous activities is at hand to amuse you this morning, from flights over Milford Sound to sailing on the lake. These are followed in the afternoon by a tour around a sheep farm.

Day 12: Lake Wanaka to Queenstown
54 km (34 miles); 3 hours cycling

An easy day's ride to finish follows the Clutha River to Cromwell before picking up the Kawarau River and barrelling through the gorge of the same name. The Kawarau Bridge is a famous venue for bungee jumping — New Zealand's answer to psychotherapy. If you have ever felt the urge to jump off a bridge, do it here with elastic attached to your feet. The

countryside opens up as you pass through the restored gold-mining settlement of Arrowtown, a few miles from Queenstown, adrenaline centre *par excellence* and the end of the road. Accommodation is in the Nugget Point Resort, in a great position overlooking the Shotover River.

Day 13: Departure

After a farewell breakfast, transfer to central Queenstown or the airport.

CONTACT:

BACKROADS

801 CEDAR STREET

BERKELEY, CA 94710-1800

USA

www.backroads.com

tel: +1 510 527 1555

The Outer Hebrides, Scotland

- Route rating: moderate
- Mainly on quiet roads; two days off-road
- 8 days/7 nights
- Dates: May, June and September

The Outer Hebrides, also known as the Western Isles, are a place apart. This 200 km (125 mile)-long archipelago is separated from mainland Scotland by a mere 50 km (30 miles) of sea, but to arrive here is to enter a different world. The weather, geography, nature, culture and language of this string of islands on the very edge of Europe, facing the might of the Atlantic Ocean, are all their own.

It is an empty place: only a handful of the 200 or more islands are inhabited, and even they have tiny populations. The landscapes are as diverse as they are unfamiliar, and from the air the islands must look like a giant camouflage jacket, so numerous are their lochs, rivers and inlets. Riding from the west to east coasts of almost any island you are likely to encounter crescent-shaped golden strands, machair (the now globally rare coastal grassland), coconut-scented gorse, squelching peat bogs and heather-wrapped mountains. Lashed by the wind and rain that familiarly curls in off the Atlantic, it looks and feels like a hard landscape for a hard people. There is nothing twee about these islands, as will be made clear from the less than prepossessing villages and homesteads you will encounter.

Yet there is also a gentleness and beauty about the Outer Hebrides that takes your breath away. At the end of the day or after a storm, they are bathed in a delicate light that changes the way you think about light for ever. You may also hear the delightful call of a corncrake, so rare now in mainland Britain. The stunning view of the mountains of North Harris from the beaches of South Harris, meanwhile, is as wonderful as any natural landscape in Scotland.

This is the northernmost extremity of the Celtic Fringe and the heart of Gaeldom: Scottish Gaelic is still widely spoken, and the fragile economy of the islands is not (at least yet) overly reliant on tourism. There is an authenticity about the place that strikes every visitor.

Dr Johnson described the Outer Hebrides as the 'rude and remote' parts of Britain. Certainly the weather can be wild and unpredictable. It is generally warm enough to wear shorts and T-shirts when cycling, but you need to keep your waterproof kit close at hand. The cycling on this trip is as varied as the weather can be, with some days spent rolling along tiny moorland roads, others involving forays into the wild mountains on jeep tracks, and several downhill blasts on tricky single-track. A support vehicle brings up the rear during the on-road days.

Whatever the weather and the ride, there will always be a warm welcome at the end of it: the islanders are renowned for their hospitality (beware if you are offered a dram of whisky, as it may not be the last), and accommodation is in friendly guesthouses. One joy of the Western Isles in the summer is that it is dark for only a few hours each night — so there is no rush to finish a ride, and there may even be time to hit the beach after dinner.

THE LIGHTHOUSE AND SEA STACKS AT THE BUTT OF LEWIS

Day 1: Arrival in Stornoway

Arrive at Inverness airport and transfer (via the ferry at Glenelg) to Skye. After lunch in the main town, Portree, cross Skye and board the evening ferry from Uig, heading out — across the Minch and into the setting sun — to Tarbert. Drive north across Harris and Lewis to Stornoway, where accommodation is in a traditional guesthouse.

Day 2: Port Nis and back to Stornoway

27 km (17 miles); 3 hours cycling

This gentle warm-up day follows the 'heritage trail' from Tolsta, along the northeast coast of Lewis to Port Nis (Port of Ness), passing seals basking on the rocks and a multitude of seabirds on the cliffs. There is also a fair chance of seeing minke whales cruising up and down the Minch. Lunch is in a charming pub in Port Nis before a trip out to see the lighthouse and the sea stacks on the Butt of Lewis. The windswept strands littered with flotsam and jetsam may inspire a spot of beachcombing before you hop into the vehicle for the drive back to Stornoway.

Day 3: Stornoway to Tarbert, via Callanish and Great Bernera

56 km (35 miles); 5 hours cycling

The ride heads west on a quiet single-track road, across the empty blanket bog that dominates the landscape of north Lewis, to Breasclete, where you continue northwards along the loch to the broch or fort at Doune Carloway. The Atlantic coast of Scotland is peppered with hundreds of these fortified towers dating from Roman times, but this one is uniquely well preserved: you cannot miss it, perched dramatically on a rocky outcrop above the sea. A little further on is the Black House Museum, offering a fascinating glimpse of 19th-century life in the Hebrides. Then it is back to Callanish for lunch and a tour of the standing stones, one of the most remarkable archaeological (and still unexplained) sites in Britain, in a superb setting. In the afternoon the ride heads out, via a causeway, to the island of Great Bernera, where you will find a small museum and a teashop at Breacleit (confusingly close in spelling to Breasclete across the water). The end of the ride (and the end of the world, some might say) comes at Bostadh, the extraordinary site of an Iron Age village, unearthed from the sand dunes by a storm in 1992. A one-hour transfer brings you back to the relative civilization of Tarbert, on the Isle of Harris.

Day 4: Loop around An Cliseam and back to Tarbert

40 km (25 miles); 5 hours cycling

This is a day of exciting mountain biking in the mighty hills of North Harris. Turning off the road from Tarbert to Huisinis at Miabhaig, you head into wild countryside, following a drover's track between the pyramid peaks of Oireabhal and Uisgneabhal. There are three tough climbs and three exciting downhills today as you loop around the back of An Cliseam, at 799 m (2,621 ft) the highest mountain in the Outer Hebrides, and along the shore of Loch Langabhat — a large body of water that stretches into the watery heart of Lewis. Golden eagles inhabit these mountains, and there is a good chance of spotting one. The final downhill of the day, a 6-km (4-mile) white-knuckle burn up, brings you out on the main road, where the vehicle will be waiting to take you back to Tarbert.

Day 5: Circuit through Reinigeadal and back to Tarbert

45 km (28 miles); 4½ hours cycling

This circular route takes in the south-eastern corner of North Harris, an area of outstanding beauty. First stop is the island of Scalpay (now reached by a causeway) before you double back for a few miles to pick up the drovers' track to Lochanan Lacasdail. This is a wonderful road, cutting down a valley to the village of Maraig. A new tarmac road then whirls down to the remote and beautiful hamlet at Reinigeadal, a great spot to rest and watch the sea. The riding gets technical now, with a single-track path along the shore of Loch Trolamaraig followed by a hefty climb (you will be pushing!) to Tharsuinn. Superb views over the mountains and across the sea back to Skye are your reward. One last section of exhilarating single-track lands you back in Tarbert.

THE WEST COAST OF THE ISLE OF LEWIS, RIMMED WITH SURF

Day 6: Tarbert to the Pollachar Inn, South Uist

56 km (35 miles); 4 hours cycling

You cover a long stretch of the archipelago today, on your steed or in the comfort of the vehicle: a combination that makes it possible to ride as much or little as you like and also duck the worst of the weather. The first transfer, from Tarbert through South Harris to the ferry at Leverburgh, passes some superb mountain and beach scenery. You start pedalling on Berneray (a holiday haunt of Prince Charles), cross to North Uist, and wend your way — past more golden beaches fringed with white-tipped breakers — to Lochmaddy for lunch. There are standing stones and nature reserves (greylag geese breed on South Uist) to attend to in the afternoon before the final transfer to the hotel overlooking the Sound of Barra.

A TRADITIONAL HEBRIDEAN STONE-BUILT COTTAGE

A DOWNHILL BLAST ON A JEEP TRACK, OUTER HEBRIDES

Day 7: Pollachar Inn to Castlebay, Barra
48 km (30 miles); 5 hours cycling

Most of the day is spent on Barra, a little gem of an island at the southern end of the archipelago, that contains a bit of everything the Western Isles have to offer. You nip over the causeway to Eriskay (the setting for Compton Mackenzie's marvellous book *Whisky Galore!*) and catch the small ferry to Barra. The airport here uses the beach for a runway (timetables roll with the tide), and you can stop in the terminal for a cup of tea. Barra is very quiet and its one road, which circles the island, is delightful. Depending on the weather, you can meander down the west coast, past more glorious beaches and through machair (listen out for corncrakes) and dunes, or follow the rocky east coast. All roads lead to Castlebay (the old herring port), where

accommodation is in a quiet, family-run B&B. If you are still full of running, you can pedal over the causeway connecting Barra to Vatersay, the last inhabited island in the archipelago. Castlebay has a couple of good pubs and is beautifully set around a cove with a medieval fortress on an islet in the water: a fitting place to end this Hebridean journey.

Day 8: Departure

Catch the ferry from Castlebay to Oban.

CONTACT:

MOUNTAIN BEACH

13 CHURCH STREET

RUDDINGTON

NOTTINGHAM NG11 6HA

UK

www.mountain-beach.co.uk

tel: +44 (0)1159 215065

The Cape and Winelands,
South Africa

- Route rating: moderate
- On-road
- 12 days/11 nights
- Dates: August to January

From the golden beaches of False Bay to the vast plain of the Little Karoo, via the mountains and vineyards of the winemaking region, the scenery of the Western Cape is staggering, and the variety of landscapes on this trip is remarkable. Add to this the chance to stand on the southernmost tip of the African continent, spot whales in the ocean, swill excellent wines and explore vibrant Cape Town, and you will understand why South Africa is the perfect destination for a long bike ride.

Most of this trip is on excellent tarmac roads, with a few short stretches of dirt track in the wine regions and on Cape Agulhas. For the most part these roads are quiet, allowing you to pedal safely while enjoying the drama of the landscape. A number of vehicle transfers are incorporated to maximize these opportunities. The ride includes a few well-graded, gentle climbs crossing the mountain ranges that divide the coastal regions from the elevated interior, but these are rewarded by fine descents, and there is always a vehicle on hand to gather up anyone who runs out of puff. The highlight of the riding, however, is beside the ocean: the sections from Hermanus to Gordon's Bay and along Chapman's Peak Drive will furnish you with sweet memories for years to come.

The daily temperatures are just right for touring, and sunshine is virtually guaranteed. Partly for this reason, the flora and fauna of the Western Cape are plentiful and varied: you will scarcely have to move from your saddle to see penguins, whales, seals, zebra, baboons, myriad sea birds and enough species of plants to send an amateur botanist into paroxysms of delight.

An additional feature of this ride is the historical perspective it will offer you. From Cape Town (the site of the first European settlement to supply passing ships in the mid-17th century), you journey inland to Stellenbosch (where early settlers acquired land for agriculture from the Hottentots) and then on into the mountains (which the Boers crossed in the 19th century on their 'Great Trek' into the interior). Castles stand as reminders of the Boer War, and slum townships as grim legacies of the years of apartheid. South Africa is a fascinating country in flux, and this journey brings its history vividly into focus.

VINEYARDS NEAR STELLENBOSCH

A MOUTH-WATERING VIEW OF TABLE MOUNTAIN

Day 1: Arrival in Cape Town

Arrive in Cape Town and transfer to a hotel by the Victoria & Albert Waterfront, a redevelopment of the old fishing harbour at the heart of the city. Here you are briefed about the trip while the bikes are assembled.

Day 2: Loop around the Cape Peninsula
55 km (35 miles); 4 hours cycling

Rather than battle it out on the streets of Cape Town, the day begins with a 30-minute transfer to the seaside resort of Muizenberg, overlooking False Bay. Then it is into the saddle for a pedal down the eastern side of the peninsula, through the towns of Fish Hoek and Simon's Town (a British naval base in the 19th century), both resonant of South Africa's colonial history. After a rest stop to admire the penguin colony at Boulders Beach, the road leads into the Cape Point Nature Reserve, home to an extraordinary diversity of plant life. This wild stretch of country offers magnificent views back towards Cape Town and Table Mountain, and over the watery immensity that rolls away south to Antarctica. A short transfer brings you to the east coast of the peninsula for a spectacular ride along Chapman's Peak Drive, arriving in Camp's Bay at cocktail hour to end a fantastic day.

Day 3: Cape Town to Stellenbosch
40 km (25 miles); 3 hours cycling

Another short transfer out of the city to Bloubergstrand (for the iconic Table Mountain vista) kicks off the day. The ride then crosses rolling green countryside fringed by blue-shadowed, craggy mountains to reach the ultra-charming town of Stellenbosch, the second-oldest town in South Africa. While it boasts an acclaimed university and a wealth of architecturally interesting buildings, its fame rests primarily on its main industry: wine. After dropping bags and bikes at the hotel, you can spend the afternoon touring vineyards (in the vehicle) and searching, via the happy process of trial and error, for the region's most elegant pinotage.

Day 4: Stellenbosch to Franschhoek
40 km (25 miles); 2½ hours cycling

You can ride (or rest your calves in the bus) to the top of Hellshoogte (Hell's Heights Pass), which offers great views of orchards, vineyards, mountains and the plains of the interior. A thrilling 15-km (9-mile) free-wheel brings you back down to the dramatic Franschhoek Valley. Almost every side road leads to a vineyard (including the Boschendal winery and its beautiful 'Cape Dutch' estate house), and you are free to explore, visit the vineyards and even sample tastings along the way throughout the afternoon. Huguenots expelled from France were some of the first settlers here, and their industry is commemorated in the museums and memorials in the town of Franschhoek — a lovely place for a wander. Accommodation for tonight is in cottages in the town, and dinner is a 'breya' or South African barbecue, doubtless accompanied by some fine local wines.

JACKASS PENGUINS ON BOULDERS BEACH

Day 5: Franschhoek to Barrydale
76 km (47½ miles); 6 hours cycling

This is a big day's ride and a chance to really stretch your legs. It begins humbly with a three-hour transfer into and along the Breede River Valley. The ride begins at Kogmans Kloof, a picturesque sandstone gorge guarded by a British Boer War fort that leads out to the quaint 'tea and scones' town of Montagu. The first white settlers passed this way to reach the Little Karoo, a broad, elevated and fertile plain bordered by the Swartberg range to the north and the Langeberg Mountains to the south. From the bottom, the climb up on to the Tradouws Plateau looks tougher than it is, and the views are superb. Then it is down quiet, country roads to the village of Barrydale and a quirky B&B with lovely gardens. Nothing much happens in Barrydale, as it is well away from the tourist trail and offers a glimpse of life in rural South Africa.

Day 6: Barrydale to Swellamdam
45 km (28 miles); 4 hours cycling

A short, well-graded climb leads over the Tradouws Pass. The descent, through the Langeberg Mountains to the restored missionary village of Suurbrak, is delightful. Lunch is in Swellamdam, the Dutch East India Company's third settlement. Afterwards you hop back in the vehicles for the short drive to Bontebok National Park, a sanctuary for rare antelope, mountain zebras, some interesting birds and a wealth of plants, which you can explore on self-guided walking trails.

APPROACHING TRADOUWS PASS IN THE LANGEBERG MOUNTAINS

Day 7: Swellamdam to Cape Agulhas
45 km (28 miles); 4 hours cycling

A one-hour transfer brings you into the Overburg District and the rolling farmland of the Western Cape. A flat, rocky bank — one of the richest fishing grounds in the world — stretches out into the ocean, and you pass a number of remote fishing villages where artists mingle with the old men of the sea. Cape Agulhas, the southernmost point of the African continent, is now a nature reserve reaching out to sea. Thousands of sea birds and seals can be seen on the untamed beaches, one of which (weather permitting — it can be wild down here) is a good spot for a picnic and a swim in the crystal-clear waters. Then it is on to the Cape Lighthouse and monument, where you can have your photo taken to prove that you have pedalled all the way from Cairo!

Day 8: Cape Agulhas to Hermanus
55 km (35 miles); 4 hours cycling

For many people, this day (and most notably spotting southern right whales from the window of a hotel in the attractive resort town of Hermanus) is a highlight of the trip. A two-hour transfer early in the morning takes you on dirt roads across the empty countryside of the Agulhas Plain. The ride alongside the Indian Ocean begins at Gansbaai, and you arrive in Hermanus in the early afternoon. The southern right whales come here to calve, oblivious to the furor they cause. This former fishing village is renowned

BEACH HUTS IN MUIZENBERG

for its excellent climate and 'champagne air', and its recent development has not destroyed its charm. A number of excellent seafood restaurants will tempt you for dinner.

Day 9: Hermanus to Gordon's Bay
90 km (56 miles); 6 hours cycling
This is the longest day in the saddle and the best – starting with a sublime ride along the violet cliffs overlooking the shining waters of False Bay, with the Cape of Good Hope beyond. Road riding rarely gets better than this. On the way you pass through a few fishing villages and nature reserves and encounter troupes of Cape baboons lounging on the road. There are several good surf beaches on False Bay, though the water is

affected by the Atlantic currents in winter and consequently can get very cold. Your hotel for the night stands on the outskirts of Gordon's Bay, another popular town with a large marina.

Day 10: Gordon's Bay to Muizenberg
45 km (28 miles); 3½ hours cycling
The ride to Muizenberg completes the circle (this is where the trip began), and to reach it you have to cross the Cape Flats townships, enormous slum settlements that sprang up during the days of the apartheid system. The beach at Muizenberg is famous for its surfing and swimming, and you can easily spend time and while away a few sybaritic hours here before transferring back to central Cape Town.

Day 11: Cape Town
You have a free day today to explore the city on bikes or by bus. There is plenty to see and do.

Day 12: Cape Town
A day for a trip to Robben Island, last-minute shopping, a surfing lesson, or just lazing in the sunshine. Transfer to the airport for the evening flight.

CONTACT:
EXODUS TRAVELS
GRANGE MILLS
WEIR ROAD
LONDON SW12 0NE
UK
www.exodus.co.uk
tel: +44 (0)870 240 5550

Cudillero to Santiago de Compostela, Spain

- Route rating: moderate
- An even mix of off-road (farm tracks) and country roads
- 8 days/7 nights
- Dates: April to October

As the saying goes, there are as many ways to Santiago de Compostela as there are places to start from. In other words, you can choose how you come and by what route, but come you must. And though there is something instantly rewarding about following a path that footsore pilgrims have travelled for hundreds of years, nowadays the appeal of this ancient journey reaches far beyond the Christian faithful. This Spanish trip, along the rugged Asturian coast and across the empty countryside of Galicia, is as much about enjoying the landscapes, culture and food as it is about the absolution of sins.

In the summer the most famous route to Santiago, the Camino Francés, is like a superhighway for pilgrims. This trip follows the last section of the much less popular Camino del Norte – an excellent choice as you travel through two regions that remain steadfastly independent from Spain. With their distinct musical traditions and their Celtic heritage, the Galicians and the Asturians look towards the sea rather than inland for their inspiration. The architecture, customs, languages and weather here all conspire to make them uniquely interesting places to pedal through.

Cycling on the Camino del Norte is evenly split between hard-packed, vehicle-width dirt tracks that meander across farmland and through forests and quiet, back-country tarmac roads with little or no traffic. There are a few hills (and the odd push), but nothing to cause any pain that cannot be assuaged by a mug of excellent Galician beer and a plate of tapas. The ride is unguided, so you follow the comprehensive trip notes provided and the scallop-shell waymarkers that indicate the Camino. There is, however, a support vehicle that transports your luggage and loiters nearby to assist with any repairs. All you need to carry, really, are a spare tube and a rain jacket (there is a reason why Galicia is so green).

Accommodation is in a mixture of small hotels and pilgrims' hostels, which are basic, comfortable and clean. The Asturians and Galicians are noted for their cuisine, and throughout the trip the food is delicious. In particular, the seafood – octopus, scallops, sardines, squid, eels and mussels – is excellent and cheap. Absolution or no absolution, this is a great bike ride.

SUNSET ON THE ASTURIAN COAST

Day 1: Arrival in Cudillero

Arrive at Oviedo airport and transfer (30 minutes) to Cudillero. Lying at the bottom of a deep gorge, where pastel-coloured houses guide you down steep, cobbled streets to the tiny port, this is probably the most picturesque fishing village on the Asturian coast. There should be time to fix up the bikes in the hotel and pick up your pilgrim's passport (in which you collect stamps from town halls, bars, churches and tourist offices on the way to Santiago) before heading out for a fine seafood dinner: the lobster paella is especially memorable.

Day 2: Cudillero to Navia
59 km (37 miles); 6 hours cycling

West of Cudillero, the waymarked Camino del Norte sinks in and out of a number of forested valleys that run down from the Cordillera Cantábrica to the coast all the way to the coast. Following this section of the trail on a bicycle makes for a laborious morning. Your route takes the old road that contours gently round these valleys, and after some 25 km (15 miles) you return to the rugged coast (for which Asturias is rightly famous) and pass through Luarca, another fishing village full of character. There is a sense of languorous decay here which may not suit ardent pilgrims, but for those who are more relaxed it is worth resting a while and watching the Asturian fishermen bustle about their business. In the afternoon the Camino follows the coast, rising on to sheer cliffs 200 m (650 ft) above the ocean shooting back down to

sandy coves. There are more small fishing hamlets facing the Bay of Biscay before you finally descend to the busy port of Navia, set on the estuary of the Rio Navia. You will be ready for your cider (a speciality of Asturias) and tapas by the time you arrive.

Day 3: Navia to Vilanova de Lourenzá
65 km (41 miles); 7 hours cycling

Winding farm tracks take you from village to village across the open countryside of the Asturian littoral, criss-crossing the main road and the railway line until you reach the bustling town of Ribadeo, at the estuary of the Eo River which forms the natural border between Asturias and Galicia. Crossing the river over the great Puente de los Santos, you enter the province of Galicia, and turning your back on the sea you continue southwest. The route heads through pine and eucalyptus forests and meadows studded with rocky precipices before entering more typically undulating Galician countryside. As if to assert the individuality of Galicia from the outset, the ceramic waymarkers (the scallop-shell symbol of St James) are inverted here. You pass more signs of Galicia's otherness, including squat granite grain stores or *hórreos*, often painted blue, and stone Crucifixions with the Virgin Mary, before

reaching the day's destination, Vilanova de Lourenzá, at the bottom of a fine descent. Accommodation here is in a basic hostel, where the rooms are en suite and the home cooking is excellent.

Day 4: Vilanova de Lourenzá to Baamonde
65 km (41 miles); 6½ hours cycling

Galicia makes much of its Celtic heritage and you have only to cycle across a small part of it to appreciate why. History, blood lineage and languages aside, Galicia nevertheless manages to both look and feel Celtic. Its ubiquitous grey granite building stone and slate roofs set it apart from the rest of Spain, as does its topography: the rolling, vivid green (and often) damp hills of Galicia are more reminiscent of Ireland than Iberia. Today's ride starts with a climb up out of Lourenzá, followed by a good descent down to the ancient town and former provincial capital of Mondoñedo. An impressive cathedral on a fine, if slightly down-at-heel, main square might well tempt you off your bike for an hour here. Then the Camino heads back into remote countryside, through forests, past small farms and more *hórreos*, over medieval bridges and on to Baamonde, where tonight's accommodation is in a small roadside hostel, again with fine local food.

THE CAMINO DEL NORTE FOLLOWS THE RUGGED

COASTLINE AS FAR AS RIBADEO

Day 5: Baamonde to Arzúa
61 km (38 miles); 5½ hours cycling

The day starts with a few kilometres along a main road, but you regain your equanimity very quickly at the turn-off. Standing at the junction is a church with a holy spring reputed to cure pilgrims with speech impediments – a throwback to the beliefs of the pre-Christian Celts. What the spring cannot do is assist any ailing cyclists up the next steep section: a 30-m (100-ft) push or a carry through quiet forests of pine. A section of easy single-track then leads out on to moorland tufted with ferns and gorse. Lunch is in Sobrado dos Monxes, an unprepossessing hamlet with a Cistercian monastery at its heart. The religious buildings were allowed to fall into a desperate state of disrepair in the 19th century, but the façade and cloisters have now gradually been restored and are certainly worth a visit. From here the Camino del Norte meanders along more country lanes and through mature woodland before heading into the busy town of Arzúa. At this point the route joins the more popular and congested Camino Francés, and the pace of life moves up a gear. Santiago is now close, and there is a real hubbub of anticipation among the massed ranks of pilgrims here. Arzúa can be a lively town at night.

Day 6: Arzúa to Santiago de Compostela
37 km (23 miles); 3½ hours cycling

On a summer's day as many as a thousand souls may make their way from Arzúa to Santiago, on foot, bicycle or horseback. The ride is predominantly downhill, with two climbs. One of these scales Monte do Gozo, where you glimpse that famous first view of the Catedral de Santiago. Even in the mêlée, it is a thrilling moment. Then it is downhill all the way, crossing the Rio Lavacolla, to reach the city. You arrive at lunchtime, collect your Compostela (pilgrim certificate), touch your forehead on the central pillar of the Portico de la Gloria and embrace the gilded bust of St James in the Romanesque basilica. Your pilgrimage complete, you can enjoy the culture and cuisine of this remarkable city.

Day 7: Santiago de Compostela

Take the morning to rest, then explore the medieval streets and splendid architecture of the old part of the city, before heading to the famous 'Parador National Hostal de los Reyes Catolicos' for a celebratory Galician feast.

Day 8: Departure

There is an opportunity to attend mass in the cathedral before transferring to the airport for the flight home.

CONTACT:

EXODUS TRAVELS

GRANGE MILLS

WEIR ROAD

LONDON SW12 0NE

UK

www.exodus.co.uk

tel: +44 (0)870 240 5550

THE GREAT, ROMANESQUE CATHEDRAL IN

SANTIAGO DE COMPOSTELA

Cappadocia to Istanbul, Turkey

- Route rating: moderate
- On-road
- 15 days/14 nights
- Dates: March to May, September to October

Turkey is vast in every sense: geographically, culturally, architecturally, gastronomically and historically. For the first-time visitor it can be a difficult country to get a handle on, but this superb trip offers you ample opportunity to do so. It is extensive in its scope. The journey starts among the cream-coloured dwellings of Cappadocia and ends in the 'Queen of Cities', Istanbul. Along the way, it explores the influence of Christianity and Islam, travels (culturally) from East to West and from Asia to Europe, advances from ancient to modern and progresses from mountains to the beach.

There are so many sights to take in during this two-week taster of Turkey; the list of highlights of the trip might include Kaymakli in Cappadocia, Konya (the spiritual capital of Turkey), Roman ruins on the Mediterranean, Kas, the Saklikent Gorge, Ephesus, Troy, ferrying across the Dardanelles, the cemeteries at Gallipoli and the bazaars of Istanbul — but it could just as easily include others. And I haven't even mentioned the cycling.

The Taurus Mountains, the Lycian coast and the rolling countryside of central Anatolia provide ample opportunity for excellent pedalling. There are some challenging days, on a road surface that is predominantly tarmac, with a few sections of graded gravel roads. The daily average distance is roughly 60 km

(37 miles), and a useful support vehicle (loaded with drinking water, trail snacks and fruit) is ever-present so you can ride as much or as little you like. To make this extensive journey possible, and to get the best out of the cycling, there are a number of vehicle transfers included in the trip.

Although Turkish cuisine is synonymous in the West with less than salubrious late-night kebab shops, the food in Turkey is excellent. Away from the tourist mêlée that has come to dominate the south-eastern corner of the country, lunches and some dinners are taken in *lokantas*, or local restaurants where you get a true flavour of the enthusiastic hospitality that is a traditional Turkish trait, as well as authentic and delicious nosh.

HAGIA SOFIA, ISTANBUL

Day 1: Arrival in Ürgüp

Arrive at Kayseri airport (via Istanbul) and transfer (1 hour) to a hotel in the market town of Ürgüp in the Cappadocia area, for briefings and a relaxing evening.

Day 2: Loop through Cappadocia
50 km (31 miles); 3½ hours cycling

There is not too much time in the saddle, but this is still a full-on day as there is so much to see. The first ride takes in some quintessential elements of the geographically improbable area of Cappadocia. The tour of this unique and bizarre lunar landscape, carved out of compacted volcanic ash, includes troglodyte villages, fairy chimneys, a complete underground monastery at Göreme and the fortress at Uçhisar. There is a stop to admire the 4,000-year-old pottery-making techniques in Avanos, famous for the quality of its onyx, before returning to Ürgüp.

Day 3: Cappadocia to Aksaray
95 km (59 miles); 6 hours cycling

The route heads south away from the main sites of Cappadocia and the tourist throng to Kaymakli, a little-visited underground troglodyte city and an excellent example of the rock-hewn architecture of the region. Then it is onward, across vast wheat fields majestically encircled by snow-capped mountains. The scenery grows even more dramatic during the afternoon, as you pedal through coppices of poplar and willow and into the red sandstone Ihlara canyon, where some of the least-visited villages and fresco-decorated, rock-cut churches. break up the afternoon ride.

Day 4: Aksaray to Beysehir
75 km (47 miles); 5 hours cycling

The day starts with a transfer to the well-preserved Selçuk caravanserai of Sultanhani. Situated a day's journey apart, caravanserais — a common feature of the central Anatolian landscape — were the motels of the ancient pan-Asian caravan or trade routes. Within their walls were mosques, accommodation, baths and stables. Rolling roads, through forests of scented pine, surrounded again by huge peaks, bring you to your next destination of Konya, a city with a wealth of Selçuk architecture and a centre of Sufi mysticism. From here, there is a transfer to Beysehir, positioned beside a vast freshwater lake with a large bird population.

Day 5: Beysehir to Side
80 km (50 miles); 3 hours cycling

Today begins with a 45-minute vehicle transfer that brings you to the top of a 1,400-m (4,600-ft) pass in the Taurus Mountains, the impressive towering range that stretches from here to Fethiye and the Turquoise Coast. It is now a fun downhill ride nearly all the way to the coast, and the exotic and ancient town of Side. Founded by the Greeks in 600 BC, Side grew rich on the slave trade. There is a wonderful theatre to explore, among other ruins, though the beach and the Mediterranean Sea may prove equally enticing. Side — being a popular resort in midsummer — has a wealth of cheap, good restaurants from which to choose for dinner.

Day 6: Side to Antalya
50 km (31 miles); 3 hours cycling

A 30-minute transfer brings you to Aspendos, the perfectly preserved Roman theatre where performances are still held today. This is a very picturesque corner of the country, and the ride through Köprülü Kanyon National Park, past Roman bridges and aqueducts to reach Serik and the coast again, is highly memorable. Another short transfer brings you to Antalya, the stunningly situated city on the Mediterranean. The hotel is in the old part of town, and you can indulge your taste for Turkish food further in one of the restaurants on the harbour.

Day 7: Antalya to Kas
40 km (25 miles); 2 hours cycling

This is a fantastic day in the saddle. A 45-minute transfer lifts you high up into the mountains, from where there are magnificent views of Antalya and the shining sea beyond. A good but quiet tarmac road leads through the snow-capped peaks of the Bey Daglar range, past villages that have scarcely been touched by the 20th century. Lunch is taken in Altinyaka, and then it is a lovely free-wheel down to Kumluca. There is an optional coast ride you could fit in before a transfer to Kas.

Day 8: Day in Kas

Modern tourism has reached Kas, but this ancient port has managed to retain much of its character. There are many ways to idle away this rest day: visit the Greek theatre on the peninsula, admire the

ROCK-CUT DWELLINGS IN CAPPADOCIA

architecture on a stroll around the town, sea-kayak in the sheltered bays and inlets, go diving, take a boat trip to explore the coast or lounge around in one of the many bars.

Day 9: Kas to Dalyan
60 km (37 miles); 5 hours cycling

The ride out of Kas along the coastal road (past Kaputas beach, a great swimming spot) eventually leads up and away from the Mediterranean. It is hard work cycling in places, but the support vehicle is ever at hand. Then it is down through glorious countryside to the Saklikent Gorge, one of the geographical wonders of the Taurus Mountains. There is plenty of time to explore, dine in one of the restaurants beside the river or plunge into a mud bath. With luck, the one-hour transfer to Dalyan will arrive in time for you to catch the stunning sunset boat trip to Isuzu beach.

Day 10: Ephesus

The whole day is spent at Ephesus, one of the greatest cities of Roman times. The ruins are vast — the population was 300,000 — and (though the temple of Diana, one of the Seven Wonders of the Ancient World, was destroyed) there is a huge amount that has been very well preserved. Walking up the main street, the 'Arcadiane', a 550-m (600-yd) sweeping marble road, is as close as you will get to time-travelling outside the Tardis. When your legs are weary, there is a transfer to the bustling and interesting town of Bergama.

CYCLISTS ON THE ROAD TO TROY

Day 11: Bergama to Assos
60 km (37 miles); 4½ hours cycling

There is an early start today to catch the sunrise at the Acropolis above the town. The ride that follows is predominantly downhill, on back roads, through pistachio forests and olive groves, with views over the Aegean Sea to the Greek island of Lesbos. To avoid a section of the busy main coast road, you hop in the vehicle for the last hour to the unspoilt, ancient fishing village of Assos.

Day 12: Assos to Çanakkale
62 km (39 miles); 5½ hours cycling

Again, the cycling is on quiet roads, through picturesque villages built from local stone. Lunch is in Alexandria Troas, a huge archaeological site, before a transfer to Troy. There is little in the way of ruins here, but it remains an atmospheric spot. The modern world is now fast encroaching on you: Çanakkale, the day's destination, is a Westernized university town with an upbeat feel.

Day 13: Çanakkale to Istanbul
27 km (17 miles); 2 hours cycling

This is a big day for many reasons. It starts with a 20-minute ferry ride across one of the world's most famous stretches of water, the Dardanelles, to enter Europe and reach the Gallipoli peninsula. This is followed by a ride through the pine woods of the National Park, dedicated to the soldiers who fell in the First World War. Lunch is at the Helles memorial, before jumping aboard the vehicle for a five-hour drive along the north shore of the Sea of Marmara and into the frenzied traffic of Istanbul. The goal is the heart of the city, the Old Town.

Day 14: Istanbul

The day is spent on a guided walking tour of the main sites of this fascinating city: the Topkapi Palace, the Hippodrome, the Blue Mosque and the covered Grand Bazaar are all on the route. In the afternoon you are free to shop before a final Turkish gastronomic experience.

Day 15: Departure

Pack up the bikes and transfer to Istanbul airport for the flight home.

CONTACT:
EXODUS TRAVELS
GRANGE MILLS
WEIR ROAD
LONDON SW12 0NE
UK
www.exodus.co.uk
tel: +44 (0)870 240 5550

OPPOSITE: THE ROYAL TOMBS AT CAUNUS, NEAR DALYAN

Crescent City to San Francisco
Northern California, USA

- Route rating: moderate
- On-road
- 7 days/6 nights
- Dates: September

Of the thousands of miles I have pedalled in more than 40 countries, few have been as memorable as the 53 km (33 miles) along what is known as the 'Avenue of the Giants'. The 'Giants' are coast redwoods, and they are gathered across northern California in what must be the finest stand of trees on the planet. John Steinbeck famously described them as 'ambassadors from another time'. Indeed, many of them were sprouting as the Romans were invading Britain. To cycle among them is a truly unforgettable experience.

The Avenue of the Giants (or Highway 254 as it is also known, rather more prosaically) is a two-lane tarmac road through the heart of the 51,000-acre Humboldt Redwoods State Park. Route 101, running more or less parallel to it, takes the burden of the traffic, allowing you to coast through this magical kingdom and survey its 100-m (300-ft)-plus leviathans at leisure. Many of the tallest trees on earth are here, and eyes should be directed heavenwards, looking to where the treetops puncture the sky, rather than watching the road nervously for cars.

This seven-day, 700-km (435-mile) ride, from Crescent City near the Oregon border to San Francisco, also takes in the Redwood National and State Parks, a 64-km (40-mile) stretch of woodland north of Orick bordering the Pacific Ocean and bisected by Route 101. Again, the trees are awe-inspiring. This section of forest was saved from the timber industry in an early and notable victory for Californian environmentalists in the late 1960s: reason enough to visit in itself.

The other outstanding feature of this ride is the glorious coast road, particularly the sections around Fort Bragg and Mendocino. Route 1 south of San Francisco, through Big Sur, may have bigger scenery and greater renown, but the northern Californian coastal road was made for bicycles. From Bodega Bay (where Hitchcock shot The Birds) to Rockport is a slow, edgy and aggravating drive, yet it is a cyclist's dream, with exquisite ocean views from the bluffs (and a good chance of spotting whales at the right time of year), long free-wheels and tight horseshoe coves to negotiate at speed.

Northern California is sparsely populated today, but the imprint of previous inhabitants is strong and their history lingers on, from Native American Miwoks and Pomos, Spanish explorers and Russian fur traders, to the fishermen and loggers of recent decades.

Cycle America, the operator of this tour, believes in bringing cycling to the masses, and this ride is run on a grand scale with groups of 50 plus. You either camp — in state parks and private campgrounds — or stay in motels and guesthouses. September, when the days are warm and the evenings cool, is the ideal time of year, but remember that the redwoods thrive on the damp climate here: it can rain hard. Breakfast and dinner are organized for you at restaurants and diners of note. The daily distances are long and there are some big hills to climb — you do need to be in good physical shape — but the ride is fully supported with vehicles, a mobile mechanic and a physiotherapist, who is on call each evening to iron out any strains.

On the final leg of the ride, you pedal 3 km (2 miles) across the Golden Gate Bridge to reach San Francisco. Coasting 67 m (220 ft) above San Francisco Bay, drinking in the stunning views of the city skyline and the headlands, you may wonder if there is a more dramatic end to a bike ride anywhere.

RUGGED COASTLINE OF BOWLING BALL BEACH, MENDOCINO COUNTY

Day 1: Crescent City to Eureka
128 km (80 miles); 7 hours cycling

The large group gathers in the morning in Crescent City and, having checked bikes and collected maps, rolls off south in dribs and drabs. By northern Californian standards Crescent City is an unprepossessing town, but after only a few miles you are into the Redwoods National Park and the first tightly packed grove of these mighty trees. Early in the morning, before the sunlight has penetrated the canopy, the air in the forest is cool and thick, enveloping you as you pedal down the undulating road. At this time of day it is not hard to understand why Native Americans saw these forests as the domain of spirits. The route follows lots of small roads that take you away from Highway 101, down to the glorious coast, and inland across fertile plains where you are likely to see elk grazing. The visitor centre at the southern end of the park stands near the Tall Trees Grove, where you can see the 112-m (368-ft) Howard Libby Redwood, the world's tallest tree. The campground is just north of Eureka, now a large industrial town. The old town and docks area (built by 19th-century timber barons) has recently been revived, and this is where you head for dinner.

Day 2: Eureka to Garberville
126 km (79 miles); 6½ hours cycling

You pedal through Eureka and around Humboldt Bay for breakfast at the Samoa Cookhouse, an old-fashioned pancakes-and-coffee diner that used to feed hungry lumberjacks. Following the back roads through small communities and towns, you come to the beginning of the fabled Avenue of the Giants. The road – which is thankfully too small for trucks or large RVs – meanders delightfully through these sky-scraping trees. There are plenty of information posts and short walking trails that take you deeper into the forest. The avenue takes up nearly half of the day, and every mile of it is to be savoured. The campground is on Dean Creek, near Garberville, once the marijuana-growing capital of northern California. The night skies are magnificent in this sparsely populated area with minimal light pollution.

COAST REDWOODS – THE TALLEST TREES ON THE PLANET

Day 3: Garberville to Fort Bragg
109 km (68 miles); 5½ hours cycling

You pass through Garberville shortly after breakfast, but the fine smell of fresh coffee and pastries might well halt your progress for another half-hour. A series of quiet backroads keep you off Highway 101 as far as the point where Route 1 breaks away and heads back towards the ocean. The first major climb of the week — and it's a big one — goes over the top of the King Mountain Range. There are fantastic views of the coastline fringed with toothpaste-white surf as you hurtle back down the serpentine road. You may recognize this stunning coastline from its many appearances in car commercials. The ride stops just short of Fort Bragg, at a state campground in a forest with walking trails down to the ocean — perfect for a moonlit walk on the beach.

Day 4: Fort Bragg to Gualala
112 km (70 miles); 6 hours cycling

In the morning this magnificent coastal ride passes through Fort Bragg and Mendocino, two towns that offer differing perspectives on the changing Californian economy. While Fort Bragg is still dominated by the logging industry, Mendocino has sold its soul to tourism. Each is interesting in its own way, but the day is really dominated by the coastal road: here you strain up through scented cypress woods to the top of bluffs and whoosh down to horseshoe coves, past sea stacks, the crashing ocean, colonies of seals and lighthouses. In the late afternoon the low sun glints on the water and illuminates the coast with a luxurious, lambent glow.

Day 5: Gualala to Duncan Mills
88 km (55 miles); 4½ hours cycling

You are nearing San Francisco now, and the fog that familiarly descends on the bay area often drifts in here in the mornings. On the long climb on a small back road that takes you away from the coast and Route 1, you might pop out above the downy fog. As this breaks up, dramatic vistas of the coast slowly emerge. In the early afternoon you hurtle back down to sea level to reach the campground at Duncan Mills, a few miles inland from Bodega Bay.

Day 6: Duncan Mills to Olema
77 km (48 miles); 4 hours cycling

This is a shorter day, so there is time to hang out in the town of Bodega, where gnarled old fishermen, followed around by gulls and pelicans, rub shoulders uncomfortably with affluent tourists. The produce of the sea is evident around Tomales Bay, and only a strong man could resist all the seafood restaurants and oyster bars that you pass. Olema is the end of the ride, though there is an opportunity to ride out to the dunes, marshes and pine-fringed ridges of the beautiful Point Reyes National Seashore before heading en masse to a restaurant for a grand final dinner.

Day 7: Olema to San Francisco
57 km (36 miles); 3 hours cycling

The population grows denser as you approach San Francisco, though this ride is arranged so that the final day is always a Sunday. There will be plenty of bikes on the road as the locals head into Muir Woods National Monument and Mount Tamalpais State Park for a morning spin. You come through Sausalito and on to the Golden Gate Bridge: riding over the bay is a fittingly dramatic finale to this ride. On the south side of the bridge the group gathers on the Presidio, the headland park, for a final picnic overlooking the bay before transferring to the airport.

CONTACT:
CYCLE AMERICA
PO BOX 485
CANNON FALLS, MN 55009
USA
www.cycleamerica.com
tel: +1 800 245 3263

THE GOLDEN GATE BRIDGE BRINGS YOU INTO SAN FRANCISCO

The Big Island, Hawaii, USA

- Route rating: easy
- On road
- 8 days/7 nights
- Dates: early November to early March

If variety really is the spice of life, then there is nowhere quite as spicy as Hawaii. Geographically, the Big Island (as it is familiarly known) has the sort of diversity that you would expect of a continent: snow-capped mountains (including the world's highest mountain measured from the sea bed), active volcanoes and lava flows, rainforests, lush ravines, prairies, deserts, sea cliffs and sandy beaches can all be found here. Climatically, the island is equally extraordinary, embracing no fewer than 11 of the world's 13 climate zones, ranging from subarctic to tropical. Add to this its amazing marine life and the colourful flora, and you will see why a tour of the Big Island is a gargantuan feast for the senses.

In stark contrast to all this diversity is the island's weather: it hardly ever changes, serving up an even 25°C (77°F) all year round on the west coast, with sunny mornings, cloudy afternoons and rain on the upper slopes. This sort of meteorological certainty ensures that the best time of year to visit Hawaii is the time when the weather is worst in your own country. If you want to see the migratory humpback whales performing their various acrobatics, though, you must come ideally between December and March, when they return from Alaska to calve in the shallow waters between the islands.

This bicycle tour is carefully arranged to reach every corner of Hawaii, but at the same time it is not too packed: there is plenty of time to snorkel, sea-kayak, bodysurf or merely get horizontal on the beach. The itinerary also makes judicious use of the island's geography: on many days you transfer to the top of the hills in the vehicle and then ride downhill. There is plenty of support and the minimum number of kilometres you have to ride each day is zero. If you want some uphill sessions (or even slightly longer distances), this can easily be arranged, but the point of this tour is to see and experience the extraordinary natural treasures of the Big Island, not to bust a gut getting to them.

THE GREEN COAST OF THE BIG ISLAND,

FRINGED WITH TOOTHPASTE-WHITE SURF

Day 1: Arrival at Keauhou Beach Resort
7 km (4 miles); ½ hour cycling

The group gathers at the Keauhou Beach Resort to meet the trip leaders, fit the bikes up and take off for a short spin. This should be finished by three o'clock, leaving time to go snorkelling (the bay has green sea turtles and clouds of colourful fish, and this is a good spot for beginners), explore the historical ruins in the grounds of the hotel, or merely kill a few hours sitting on your lanai (or porch) sipping a Mai Tai.

Day 2: Keauhou to Pu'uhonua O Honaunau
46 km (29 miles); 3½ hours cycling

A 50-minute transfer takes you up to 425 m (1,400 ft), high above the island's main town, Kailua-Kona, for the first major downhill cruise through coffee plantations to the coast. En route to Kealakekua Bay there is a working Kona coffee factory, producing the highly aromatic product of the Big Island's rich volcanic soil, where you can taste freshly brewed samples. This is also where Captain James Cook, the great explorer and the first known Westerner to visit Hawaii, died in 1779: a town and a rocky point are named after him. Kealakekua Bay itself is a state underwater park and marine life conservation area. Again, the snorkelling is excellent, and there is a good chance of spotting spinner dolphins in the water as you pedal south along the coast. The next stop is Pu'uhonua O Honaunau – now a 'historical park' and formerly a place of great spiritual significance for the islanders.

A self-guided walk takes you past the main sites (including the 17th-century heiau or temple where chiefs were buried on the point of the cove), ending up on the beach for a picnic lunch. In the afternoon, you climb (or ride in a van) up to St Benedict's, a Catholic church set in lovely gardens. Another transfer brings you again to 425 m (1,400 ft) for the freewheel down to the hotel. (Do you begin to recognize a pattern here?) In the late afternoon there is an opportunity to go sea-kayaking.

Day 3: Punalu'u Beach Park and South Point
46 km (29 miles); 3 hours cycling

An early morning transfer brings you to the Mamalahoa Highway lookout, 500 m (1,600 ft) above the southern end of the island. The wooded descent, through native ohia and koa trees and dense vegetation of myriad forms, is lush and truly lovely. This is the southeastern, windward side of the island, and it is a different world from arid but sunny Keauhou. A picnic lunch is provided on the black sand beach at Punalu'u. Afterwards, riding down South Point road in the afternoon, you may well feel awed: this is the southernmost point of the USA, but with the towering palisades and pounding ocean, it feels like you are pedalling towards the edge of the world. A short transfer takes you to your new accommodation for the night – Kilauea Lodge, a small hotel in the village of Volcano.

Day 4: Volcanoes National Park
24 km (15 miles); 4 hours cycling

A short early morning ride brings you into the fabulous and unique Volcanoes National Park. The landscape here is the stuff of fantasy: there are craters and cinder cones, hills of pumice, rivers of solidified lava, steam vents, rainforests and fern groves. First stop is the visitor centre before setting off on the Crater Rim road, a wonderful 18-km (11-mile) loop round the rim of Kilauea Caldera. Hawaiians believe this is the home of Madame Pele, goddess of volcanoes (offerings to her are left around the rim), and peering down from Halemaumau Overlook, inhaling the sulphurous fumes and watching steam blowing through the lava crust, you may well feel the presence of a spirit from another world. After lunch back at the visitor centre, you can either keep on riding (down to the winery near the village) or walk the Kilauea Iki trail across the hardened crater floor, above a lake of molten lava.

THE ROUTE LOOPS ROUND THE CALDERA OF KILAUEA VOLCANO

Day 5: Kilauea Lodge to Hilo via Keaau
37 km (23 miles); 2 hours cycling

The day begins with a 37 km (23 mile), gentle downhill cruise through a variety of climates and vegetation to Keaau, a town that still thrives on the rural economy. The lava-rich soil (the most recent eruptions in the area have been spewing lava since 1983) produces good crops of macadamia nuts, orchids, anthuriums and other tropical flowers for which the region of Puna is famous. The traffic builds up on Highway 11 as it approaches Hilo, so it is back into the vehicle for a ride into this old sugar-exporting port and the regional capital of Big Island's east coast. Hilo is an ethnically diverse town with an aged façade, having escaped the invasive modern development which characterizes Kona. It also has a reputation for survival: lava flows from the mountains and tsunamis from the sea are a constant threat. Having explored the downtown area — there are some interesting museums — you head to the Hilo Canoe Club on the bay for lunch and a trip in an outrigger canoe.

Day 6: Kilauea Lodge to Hapuna Beach
37 km (23 miles); 3½ hours cycling

The windward side of Hawaii is fissured by a number of extravagantly lush, steep-sided valleys filled with roaring water. A transfer drops you on the east coast at the start of the trail up to Akaka Falls, arguably Big Island's most impressive waterfall. The path, through the sleepy town of Honomu and into dense jungle full of bamboo groves and hanging heliconia, ends at the magical 134 m (440 ft) fall.

The next transfer is along the Hamakua Coast, beneath Mauna Kea, with views north to the island of Maui. This brings you to the town of Kamuela in the foothills of the Kohala Mountains and at the centre of the Parker Ranch, the largest private cattle ranch in the USA. From here it is downhill again on two wheels to Hapuna Beach, one of the finest beaches on Big Island. You may find it hard to leave.

Day 7: Waikoloa to Mahu Kona State Park via Pololu Lookout
22 km (14 miles); 2 hours cycling

A vehicle transfer first thing this morning takes you around the northern point of the island to the end of Highway 270 and the Pololu Lookout, from which there are superb views of chiselled cliffs plummeting into the ocean. The ride follows the Kohala Coast through the quiet towns of Kapa'au and Hawi (where the art galleries might hold you up for a while), rolling up and down and contouring around canyons thick with vegetation before opening out into what was once sugarcane country. From December to March it is possible to spot whales in the ocean between Big Island and Maui. A picnic lunch is prepared for you at Mahukona Beach Park, where the snorkelling can be excellent when the sea is calm. The final section of the ride (for those who wish) follows the course of the famous Hawaii Ironman contest.

Day 8: Departure

There is time for a swim or a final snorkel this morning before transferring back to Kailua-Kona airport for the flight home.

CONTACT:

VBT

614 MONKTON ROAD

BRISTOL, VT 05443-0711

USA

www.vbt.com

tel: +1 800 245 3868

THE WINDWARD SIDE OF HAWAII IS FISSURED BY

A NUMBER OF EXTRAVAGANTLY LUSH VALLEYS

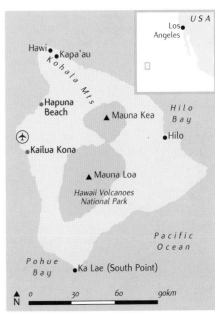

Durango to Moab,
The San Juan Hut System, USA

- Route rating: moderate
- Off-road (dirt and gravel roads)
- 7 days/6 nights
- June to late September

Mountain bikes were invented for rides like this one: a 346-km (215-mile) dirt-road adventure over the high alpine tundra of the San Juan Mountains and down into the desert canyonlands of Utah.

The ride starts in Durango, a town that has played a serious part in the short history of mountain biking. The sport may have originated in northern California, but it came to fruition here, on the web of trails that crawl over the steep slopes of the San Juan Mountains. There is a bike shop on every street corner in Durango, and a handful of world-class riders call the town home. Neon Lycra is virtually de rigueur. Not that everyone wears it: Durango is the largest town in southwest Colorado and something of a melting pot, with bikers and ranchers, tourists and hobos all rubbing shoulders here.

The destination is Moab, the outdoor activity capital of south-west USA and another mountain-biking mecca. It is not a place richly endowed with cultural highlights, but it will seem like a dazzling metropolis after your time in the wilderness. If you are not tired of riding when you get to Moab, you can take a spin on the world-famous Slickrock Trail.

For the six nights between Durango and Moab, your stay will be in huts. These huts (newly-built in 2004) are all kitted out with eight padded bunks, wood stoves, plenty of food (three good meals a day), firewood, drinking water and sleeping bags. There are composting toilets and one hut boasts a shower – the rest of the time you splash or swim in the lakes and streams.

Using high-altitude huts is nothing new in the European Alps. In the USA the idea is relatively fresh, and the application to mountain biking is even more recent, but it is a combination that works perfectly. This hut system offers an excellent balance between rough camping and luxurious pampering. Crucially, it means that you can cross this beautiful American wilderness without having to carry your tent, cooking equipment and the kitchen sink. You have to carry remarkably little, in fact: rain gear, sunblock, a fleece or jumper for the cool evenings, a sleeping-bag liner, a water filter, first-aid kit and some bike tools. All of this should fit into a small rucksack and still leave plenty of room for a camera and spare water. This is mountain-bike touring as it should be.

A little bit of comfort does not mean that the ride is short on adventure, however. The average altitude over the week is high at 2,900 m/9,500 ft, the temperature can plummet to below freezing at night, and the weather can change unpredictably. In the early autumn you can easily get caught in a snowstorm on one of the high passes. There is no vehicle support and no guide. The 346-km (215-mile) route mainly follows Forestry Service and Bureau of Land Management dirt roads. It is a serious physical workout, and you do need to be in good shape to enjoy it.

There is little or no technical cycling on the standard route – all you need is the confidence to ride on dirt trails. For aficionados of single-track riding, there are technical trails around the huts for afternoon and evening entertainment. Riders also need basic bike-maintenance skills – the chances are you will end up fixing something, somewhere beside the trail – and a basic knowledge of first aid would also be preferable. If you come fit and prepared, you are truly in for a taste of mountain-biking nirvana.

ON PORCUPINE RIM, LOOKING DOWN ONTO THE DESERT CANYONLANDS OF UTAH

Day 1: Durango to Bolam Pass Hut
29 km (18 miles); 4½ hours cycling

You should check your gear in Durango and make any last-minute purchases (trail food to get you to the first hut, for example) before heading 43 km (27 miles) north on Highway 550 (by bike or taxi) to the Durango Mountain Resort and the start of the trail. Durango is practically engulfed by the San Juan National Forest, so you are in among the pines as soon as you find the dirt road that leaves the parking lot. This is the heart of the San Juan Mountains, home to some seriously rugged terrain. There are dozens of mountain-biking trails in this area, but slowly you will leave the crowds behind. Wild flowers — lupins, globe mallows, mountain iris and many others — carpet whole hillsides in the summer months. The day is predominantly uphill, with a tough climb to reach the Bolam Pass and the hut (3,478 m/11,411 ft) at the end of it. From the hut there are superb views into the heart of the San Juan Mountains, where three peaks over 4,250 m (14,000 ft) stand proudly.

Day 2: Bolam Pass Hut to Black Mesa Hut
46 km (29 miles); 5 hours cycling

The route continues through stands of spruce, Douglas fir and ponderosa pine, but you do not feel enclosed by the forest. Huge views (the air in Colorado is famously clean) open up over the mountains back to the east as you edge closer to the tallest peaks in the range. Eventually you leave the forest behind and spill out on to the open hillside, riding just below the high alpine tundra. Elk live here, as does the more reclusive black bear. For this self-guided tour, you are provided with maps and route descriptions that detail both the standard route and harder variations. Before you get used to the terrain, however, it is easy enough to lose your way and anyone with a suspect sense of direction might want to pack a GPS (Global Positioning System). There is another long climb to get back up to 3,238 m (10,625 ft) and the second hut.

Day 3: Black Mesa Hut to
Hamilton Creek Hut
67 km (42 miles); 5½ hours cycling

This is the first day of major climatic transition, as you leave the green mountains behind and head for the high mesa, and trees and shrubs give way to sagebrush and arid grasslands. The days are now increasing steadily in intensity, with a lot of climbing and some hairy descents as you cross the canyons between the San Juan Mountains and the La Sal Mountains. On the approach to the hut you ride back into forest, but this is a desolate landscape of charred pinyon and ponderosa pines — evidence of the huge fire that tore through here in 2002.

COLORADO HAS A WEALTH OF GREAT SINGLE-TRACK TRAILS

Day 4: Hamilton Creek Hut to Wedding Bell Hut
48 km (30 miles); 4½ hours cycling

The landscape changes again today as you drop down into the distinctive, treeless Dry Creek Basin and the fearsome canyonlands: 2,500 square kilometres (1,000 square miles) of sculpted red earth that stretch far away across Utah. There are coyotes and antelope here, but you have to keep a sharp eye out to spot them. The geology, flora, fauna and even the weather are different here. The riding, however, remains excellent. The hut is dramatically positioned on the edge of a cliff that drops 600 m (2,000 ft) down to the Dolores River.

Day 5: Wedding Bell Hut to Paradox Hut
55 km (34 miles); 4½ hours cycling

You are now nearing the very heart of red rock canyon country as you head north into a lower, hotter zone dotted with cactus plants that looks like the Wild West of old: Butch Cassidy and the Sundance Kid were born here. Astonishing panoramas of mountain ridges fold away to the horizon in the dazzling sunlight. A huge drop leads to the hut, on a single-track cattle trail down a sheer cliff. Some of it is too steep to ride and you may have to struggle down on foot, but the views are correspondingly dramatic. The Paradox Hut where tonight's accommodation will be (at 1,597 m/5,240 ft the lowest altitude you sleep at all week) can be a little hot at night.

Day 6: Paradox Hut to Geyser Pass Hut
42 km (26 miles); 6 hours cycling

The La Sal Mountains — a familiar landmark by now as you have been edging towards them all week — protrude ostentatiously from the flat desert. It is now time to climb them. This is the toughest day of the week. As you ascend from Paradox Hut at 1,597 m (5,240 ft) to 3,007 m (9,864 ft), you pass through all the different types of vegetation that you have seen so far, ending up back in alpine tundra. The effort is worth it: sitting on top of some of the most remote and beautiful mountains in the USA is a great way to watch the sun go down over Utah. Enjoy the alpen glow. This hut is on private land — a vast cattle ranch where you may even bump into real cowboys out on the range — in the sub alpine zone with tundra immediately above you in all directions. There are views back to the mountains where you started the ride at the beginning of the week.

Day 7: Geyser Pass Hut to Moab
55 km (34 miles); 4 hours cycling

The last day starts with one final climb through the La Sal Mountains, across meadows and through stands of aspen and fir, to reach the saddle at Geyser Pass (3,261 m/10,700 ft). Enjoy a moment of repose here — and savour the views north towards Arches National Park and Canonlands National Park — because all hell breaks loose on the way down. This is a massive 2,130 m (7,000 ft) descent (with a number of variations to choose from) into the town of Moab. Verdant

pastures give way once again to rocky valleys as you thunder through several geological eras and into the raw heat of Utah.

CONTACT:

SAN JUAN HUT SYSTEM

PO BOX 773

RIDGWAY, CO 81432

USA

www.sanjuanhuts.com

tel: +1 970 626 3033

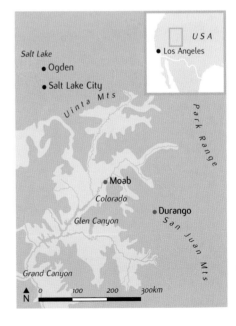

Snowdonia and the Lleyn Peninsula, Wales

- Route rating: moderate
- On-road
- 8 days/7 nights
- Dates: July to September

The northwestern corner of Wales has remained steadfastly independent for centuries. Successive invasions — by Romans, Normans, Anglo-Saxons and, more recently, English holidaymakers — have never subdued this heartland. It is here, appropriately, that the last king of Wales reigned. Snowdonia and the Lleyn Peninsula, then, are the final refuge, where the pulse of this nation can be felt most keenly even today. Welsh remains the first language of a large proportion of the population, and culturally the Cmyric identity, that indefinable 'Welshness' that remains so vital to Wales, is as intact here as it is anywhere.

The region is dominated by Mount Snowdon, the pyramid-shaped peak that sits on raised buttresses of volcanic rock and is familiarly shrouded in a mystic, iridescent light. This intense light — a result of the proximity of the sea, the type of rock and the latitude — has drawn landscape painters and more recently photographers in their droves. It is a curious thing to come here for the first time and feel that you know it, though only from images. Snowdon is a modest 1,086 m (3,560 ft) high, but its shape is that of a proud and lofty mountain. There are many glorious views of Snowdon throughout the week of this tour, and few will ever tire of seeing it.

The area comprising all the mountains in the region is called Snowdonia, or 'Eryri' in Welsh. It reverberates with rich historical associations (particularly those relating to Welsh defiance of the English) and, perhaps even more potently, it is steeped in legend. King Arthur fought his last battle here, Excalibur was thrown into a lake here and these hills are where Merlin wandered. Non-Welsh speakers often struggle to pronounce the place names at first, but by the end of the week you will be curling your tongue round names such as Llandwrog and Rhyd-Ddu like a Celtic bard of old.

The Lleyn Peninsula, which protrudes into the Irish Sea like a claw, resembles Cornwall, albeit on a smaller scale. The north coast is rugged, and the south coast has a number of arcing, sandy beaches. Seals abound in the water and the rich birdlife — cormorants, oystercatchers, gannets, guillemots and kittiwakes — is typical of the western seaboard of Britain. And, there's plenty of man's imprint on the land, from ancient standing stones to evidence of the early quarrying industry.

The cycling is pretty good, too. The week comprises a good mix of day tours on lanes, drovers' routes and cycleways, exploring the landscape and the rich cultural heritage of the area. There are two days spent traversing the edge of Snowdonia, and some tough climbing is unavoidable. Yet for this ride the routes have not been chosen for lung-splitting ascents and screaming downhills. Rather, they have been chosen because the traffic is light and there are plenty of interesting places to stop at; whether it be a tea shop, an ancient holy well, a castle, a cave, a beach, a bakery or a pub, there always seems to be a good reason to take a breather and dismount. After all, this is a 'beano' (as in the name of the company organizing the ride), an old-fashioned English slang word for a 'jolly'.

THE VIEW ACROSS NANTLLE LAKE INTO THE HEART OF SNOWDONIA

Day 1: Arrival at Trigonos

You arrive in the former slate-quarrying village of Nantlle on the western edge of Snowdonia National Park. Trigonos, your accommodation and HQ for the week, is set in more than seven hectares (18 acres) of private land beside Lake Nantlle. There is a superb view (made famous by the 18th-century British landscape painter Richard Wilson) across the water towards the eyrie of Snowdon itself. Trigonos supports a large organic vegetable garden, and much of the excellent vegetarian food that will fortify you throughout the week comes from here.

Day 2: Circular ride via Caernarfon
53 km (33 miles); 4½ hours cycling

The week starts with a gentle roll on flattish roads down to the coast and the Irish Sea. Clynnog Fawr has a fine church and an ancient holy well dedicated to St Bueno, Wales's most important saint after St David. There are views across Caernarfon Bay as you head north to Llandwrog for lunch at the Harp Inn. Then it is on, via the Iron Age hill fort at Dinas Dinlle and the Menai Straits Nature Reserve, to Caernarfon, where one of Europe's finest medieval castles, built by the English king Edward I to subdue the unruly Welsh, stands perfectly intact. After tea and a castle tour, it is back to Nantlle on lanes and the Lon Effion cycle path, stopping on the way to wonder at the vast lunar landscape of the Dorothea slate quarries, which are now derelict.

Day 3: Circular ride via Criccieth
67 km (42 miles); 6 hours cycling

Leaving Nantlle the route heads south along lanes to the small town of Criccieth. From the waterfront there is a quintessentially Welsh prospect across Porthmadoc Bay to Harlech Castle, with Cadair Idris behind. You will notice a distinct change in the scenery as you cycle along the south coast of the Lleyn Peninsula, where in contrast to the rugged north, the south consists of sandy beaches and coastal woods. Lunch is taken in the Blue China in Criccieth, which occupies a lovely spot beside the beach. There is time for a swim (the sea is not as cold as it looks) before continuing on undulating lanes to the birthplace of one of Wales's favourite sons, David Lloyd George, Prime Minister of Britain during the First World War. There are a number of options for detours for anyone who has already found their cycling legs, but alternatively, a recommended walking route brings you to another holy well where — or so the legend goes — you can test your lover's faithfulness!

Day 4: Circular ride via Llanberis
55 km (34 miles); 4½ hours cycling

Enjoy your breakfast, because the day starts with a climb — the first of four today — up the Nantlle Valley to Rhyd Ddu. You are right in among the mountains here, immediately beneath the airy heights of Snowdon. There is some respite on the top road to Bryngwyn and a coffee break (at a café run, imaginatively, by people with special needs) before more climbing over the shoulder of Snowdon. From the top the views are mighty: you can see most of the places you visit during the week. The payback is a fast descent into Llanberis where there are many places for lunch, as well as the Welsh Slate Museum and the Snowdon narrow-gauge railway. There are two further climbs on the way back to Nantlle, eased by the pleasure of stops for cake and ale.

Day 5: Free day

A day off, with time to visit the world-famous village of Portmeirion or take a ride on the Ffestiniog railway.

WATER GLIDES OFF THE ABERGLASLYN PASS

Day 6: Hell's Mouth ride
50 km (31 miles); 5 hours cycling

A 45-minute vehicle transfer brings you to the start of today's ride at the village of Tudweiliog. This is the Lleyn Peninsula proper, beyond the reach of the railway and a place apart that resonates with its own identity. The first stop, after an hour, is Whistling Sands, a pristine swimming beach with a café. Continuing on the way to the village of Aberdaron, you can take a short detour that leads on to the headland, where the gorse and heather are truly spectacular. As you reach the village there are stunning views over Bardsey Island, once a place of pilgrimage in the first centuries of Christianity in Britain. Seals are often to be seen bobbing in the swell below the headland. Lunch is in a hotel overlooking the sea among the whitewashed houses of Aberdaron. Boats to Bardsey depart from here, and the medieval pilgrims have left their mark on this small village facing the ocean. In the early afternoon the cycling gets tougher as the road climbs up Mynnydd Rhiw – the site of a Neolithic axe factory – for well-deserved panoramic views over Hell's Mouth beach. Then it is an hour's cycling back to Tudweiliog and the Lion Hotel for beverages before the transfer back to Nantlle.

MIST HANGS IN THE VALLEYS OF SNOWDONIA

Day 7: Circular ride via Beddgelert
60 km (37 miles); 5 hours cycling

This is the biggest day's riding and the last. The route sweeps around the mountains of the southwest corner of Snowdon. The first stop, after a gentle hour, is Garndolbenmaen, where there is an optional detour up Cwm Pennant, a former slate-mining valley and a famous beauty spot. Then it is up, past a working woollen mill, over the moor on an old drovers' road and down to the village of Prenteg, from which there are great coastal views. Clough Williams-Ellis, who created Portmeirion, is the dominant figure around Porthmadog, so it is appropriate to stop for lunch in Garreg, the estate village he created. You can visit the great man's house and gardens (Plas Brondanw) or walk up to the folly on the hill. The lure of an ice cream might keep you pedalling over the (oft-painted) Aberglaslyn Pass to reach Beddgelert, a pretty village and the home of the most sentimental dog grave in Wales. There is a final one-hour climb through pine forests to reach the pub at Rhyd-Ddu, and time for refreshments before descending into the Nantlle Valley as the sun sets on the 'grandeur and desolation' (as Wordsworth put it) of Snowdonia for the last time on the tour. You depart the following morning.

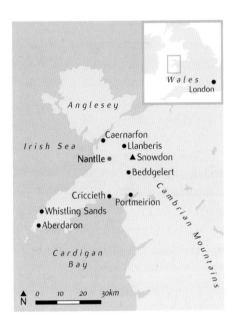

CONTACT:
BICYCLE BEANO CYCLING HOLIDAYS
ERWOOD
BUILTH WELLS
POWYS
WALES LD2 3PQ
UK
www.bicycle-beano.co.uk
tel: +44 (0)1982 560471

Index of cycling holiday companies

Numbers in *italic* indicate page references

Picture credits

The publisher would like to thank the following photographers, agencies and organizations for their kind permission to reproduce the photographs in this book:

4 Gary Pearl/Stockshot

6 David Williams/Photolibrary Wales

8 James Davis Worldwide/Eye Ubiquitous

10 Austrian National Tourist Office

11 David Cumming/Eye Ubiquitous

12–13 James Davis Worldwide/Eye Ubiquitous

14 John Warburton-Lee Photography

16 Roberto Gerometta/Backroads

17 John Warburton-Lee Photography

18 Kathy Jarvis/South American Pictures

19 Backroads (Courtesy Llao Llao Hotel)

20–24 Henry Georgi Photography

26 Paul A.Souders/Corbis

28 Chris Coe/Axiom Photographic Agency

29 Ben Davidson/Backroads

30 Jacob Taposchaner/Getty Images

32 James Davis Worldwide

34–35 Nick Haslam/Hutchison

36 Stephen Coyne/Travel Ink

38-41 David Hughes/Images of France

42 Cycling Classics

43 PA Photos/EPA

44 Paul Thompson/Eye Ubiquitous

47 James Davis Worldwide/Eye Ubiquitous

48 D.Coello/Backroads

49 David Hughes/Images of France

50 Ian Cumming/Axiom Photographic Agency

52 Steven Behr/Stockfile

53 Jeremy Phillips/Travel Ink

54 Exodus Travel

56 Keith Wood/Corbis

59-60 Peter Rayner/Axiom Photographic Agency

61 Tim Greening/KE Adventure Travel

62 Bryan and Cherry Alexander Photography

64 Harald Sung/The Image Bank/Getty Images

67 Bryan and Cherry Alexander Photography

68 Mark Hannaford/John Warburton-Lee Photography

70–72 Diego Martin/John Warburton-Lee Photography

73 Jamie Carr/KE Adventure Travel

74 and 76 Christopher Hill Photographic/Scenic Ireland

77 Northern Ireland Tourist Board

78 Christopher Hill Photographic/Scenic Ireland

80 Chris Coe/Axiom Photographic Agency

83 Joe Cornish/Getty Images

84–85 Nick Bonnetti/Eye Ubiquitous

86 Glenn Rowley/KE Adventure Travel

88 James Strachan/Getty Images

89 Tim greening/KE Adventure Travel

90 James Strachan/Getty Images

91 Mark Hannaford/John Warburton-Lee Photography

92 Andrew Errington/Getty Images

94–95 Exodus Travel

96–97 Ian Cumming/Axiom Photographic Agency

98 Chris Caldicott/Axiom Photographic Agency

100 Ian Cumming/Axiom Photographic Agency

101 Exodus Travel

102 David Guyler/Travel Ink

104 Peter Morath Photography Ltd.

106 B Tanaka/Taxi/Getty Images

107 John Warburton-Lee Photography

108 Paul Chesley/Getty Images

109 Markham Johnson/Backroads

110–114 Scottish Viewpoint Picture Library

115 Mountain Beach

116 Chris Coe/Axiom Photographic Agency

118 Frans Lemmens/Getty Images

119–120 Exodus Travel

121 John Warburton-Lee Photography

122–125 Hubert Stadler/Corbis

126 H.Marstrand/Axiom Photographic Agency

128 Christina Dameyer/Lonely Planet Images

131 Chris Barton Travel Photography

132 Robert Landau/Corbis

133 Exodus Travel

134 Wes Walker/Lonely Planet Images

136–137 Chris Barton Travel Photography

138 Neil Emmerson/Robert Harding

140 Galen Rowell/Corbis

143 Douglas Peebles/Corbis

144–145 David Muench/Corbis

146 Per Breiehagen/Getty Images

148–149 Lee Cohen/Corbis

150 David Muench/Corbis

152 Steve Lewis/Photolibrary Wales

155 Paul Kay/Photolibrary Wales

156–157 Dave Newbould/Photolibrary Wales

Every effort has been made to trace the images' copyright holders We apologise in advance for any unintentional omissions, and would be pleased to insert the appropriate acknowledgment in any subsequent printing.

Author's Acknowledgments

Thanks a million to Mum and Dad for
pushing the boat out with my first racing
bike, Dervla Murphy for providing the
inspiration to explore on two wheels,
Will Farara, Jim Cole, Andy Morley-Hall,
the inimitable Smudgers, Roberts Cycles
for building Mannanan, the puncture
gods, Vicks, Lucas, Scarlett and Katrina
for waving me off and welcoming me
home, Camilla Hornby, Sybella Marlow
and the team at Conran Octopus, and
all the people from around the world
who have been so forthcoming with the
advice and information needed to put
this book together.